Nickolas Flux HISTORY CHRONICLES

PERIL IN POMPEII!

NICKOLAS FLUX and the Eruption of Mount Vesuvius

BY Nel Yomtov
ILLUSTRATED BY Mark Simmons

CONSULTANT:
Richard Bell, PhD
Associate Professor of History
University of Maryland, College Park

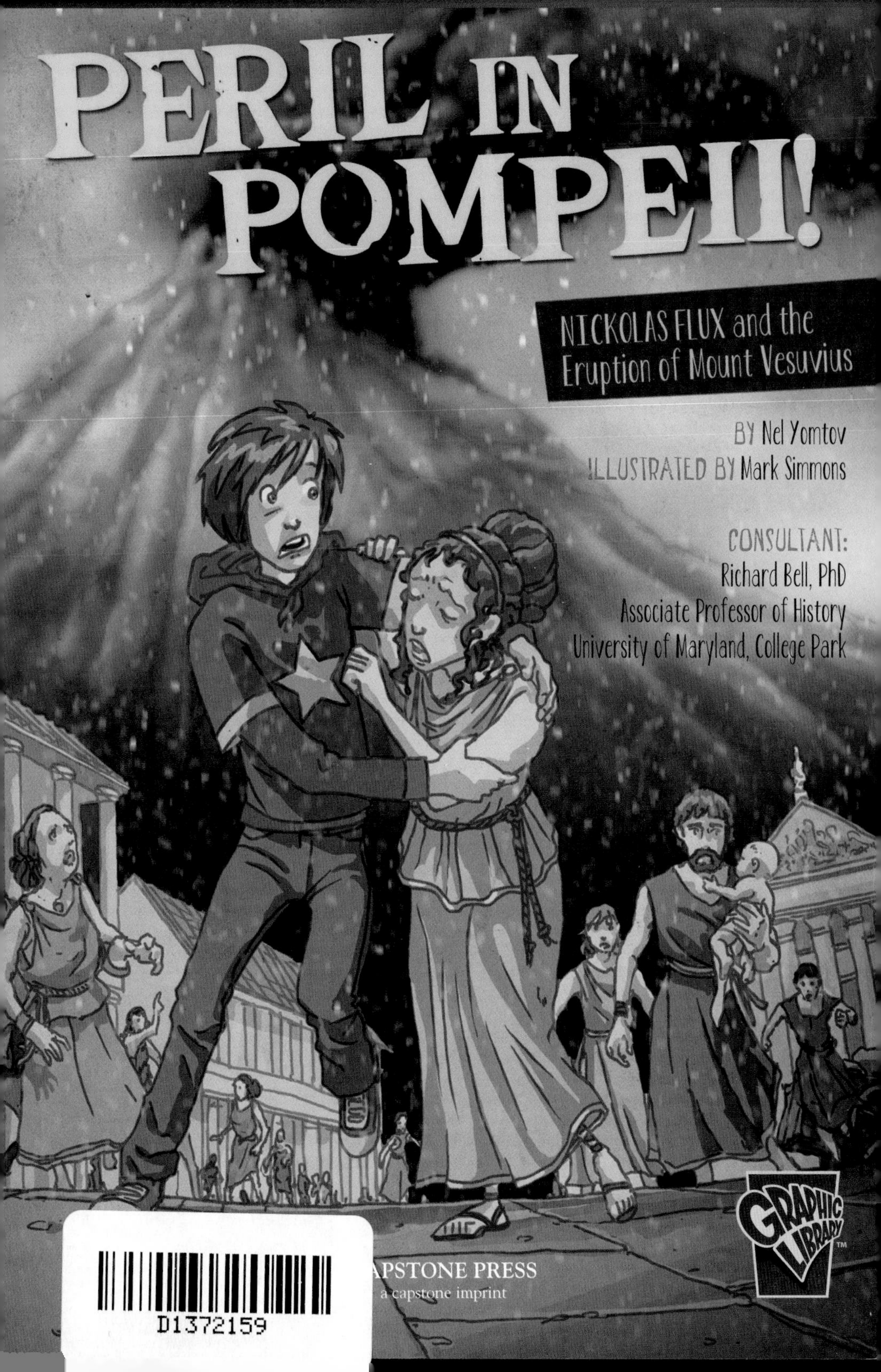

CAPSTONE PRESS
a capstone imprint

Graphic Library is published by Capstone Press,
1710 Roe Crest Drive, North Mankato, Minnesota 56003
www.capstonepub.com

Library of Congress Cataloging-in-Publication Data
Yomtov, Nelson.
  Peril in Pompeii! : Nickolas Flux and the eruption of Mount Vesuvius /
by Nel Yomtov ; illustrated by Mark Simmons.
    pages cm.—(Graphic library. Nickolas Flux history chronicles)
  Includes bibliographical references and index.
  Summary: "In graphic novel format, follows the adventures of Nickolas
Flux as he travels back in time and must survive the eruption of Mount
Vesuvius"—Provided by publisher.
  ISBN 978-1-4914-0251-1 (library binding)
  ISBN 978-1-4914-0256-6 (paperback)
  ISBN 978-1-4914-0260-3 (eBook PDF)
1. Pompeii (Extinct city)—Juvenile literature. 2. Pompeii (Extinct
city—Comic books, strips, etc. 3. Vesuvius (Italy)—Eruption, 79—
Juvenile literature. 4. Vesuvius (Italy)—Eruption, 79—Comic books,
strips, etc. 5. Graphic novels. I. Simmons, Mark, illustrator. II. Title.
  DG70.P7Y66 2015
  937.72568—dc23   2014003771

Photo Credits:
Design Elements: Shutterstock (backgrounds)

EDITOR
Christopher L. Harbo

ART DIRECTOR
Nathan Gassman

DESIGNER
Ashlee Suker

PRODUCTION SPECIALIST
Jennifer Walker

COVER ARTIST
Dante Ginevra

Printed in the United States of America in Stevens Point, Wisconsin.
032014   008092WZF14

TABLE OF CONTENTS

INTRODUCING ...

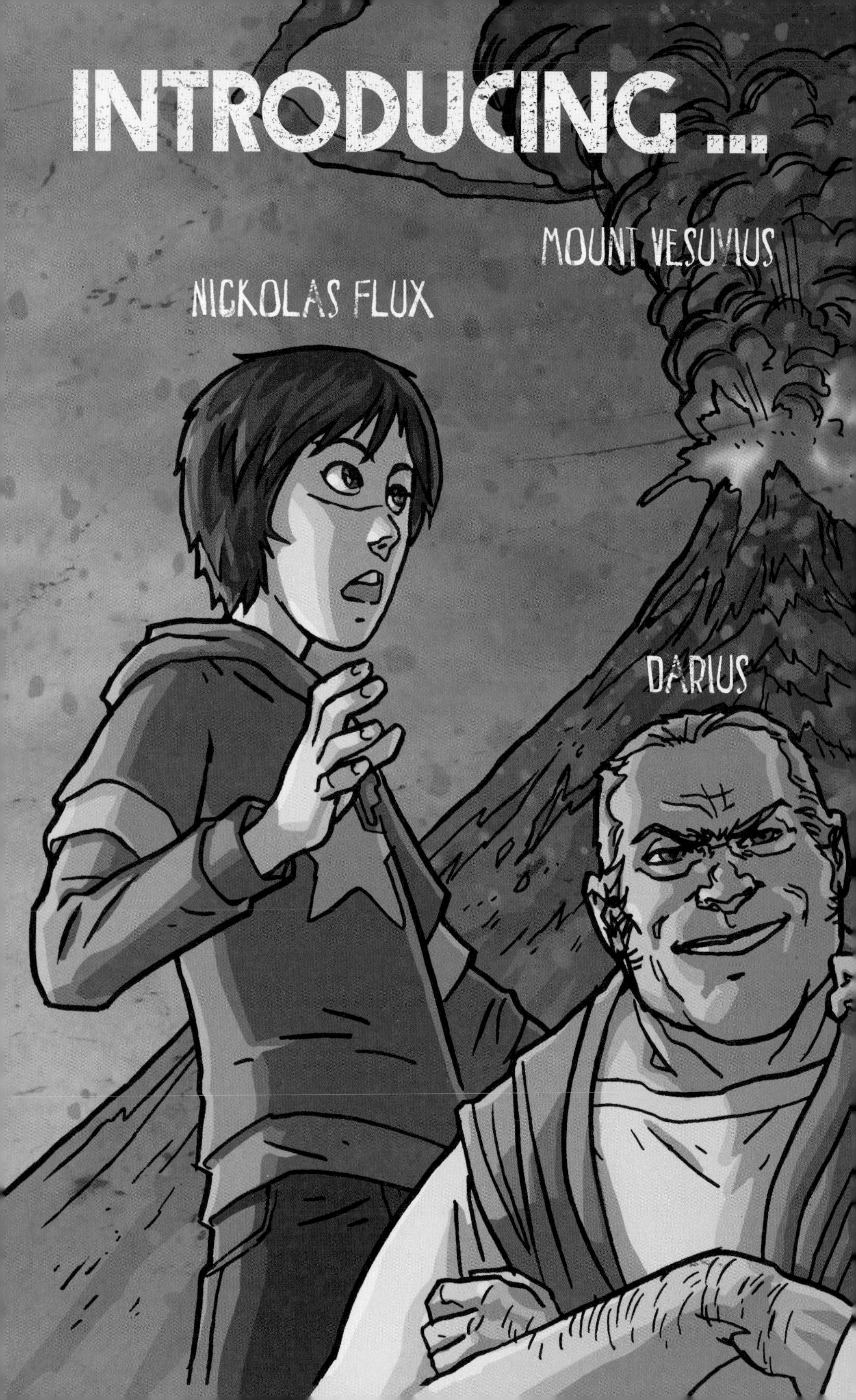
MOUNT VESUVIUS
NICKOLAS FLUX
DARIUS

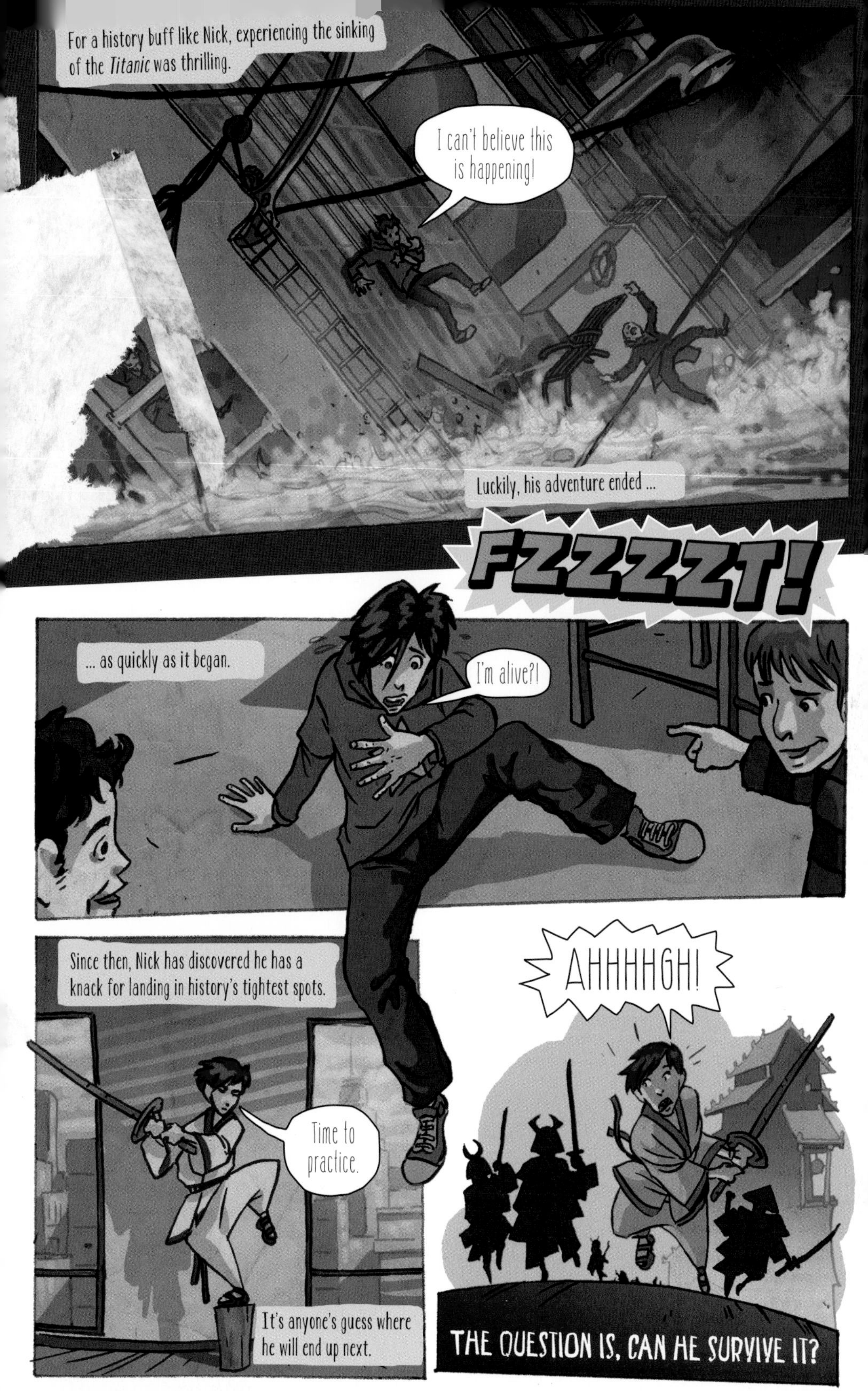
For a history buff like Nick, experiencing the sinking of the *Titanic* was thrilling.
I can't believe this is happening!
Luckily, his adventure ended ...
FZZZZT!
... as quickly as it began.
I'm alive?!
Since then, Nick has discovered he has a knack for landing in history's tightest spots.
Time to practice.
It's anyone's guess where he will end up next.
AHHHHGH!
THE QUESTION IS, CAN HE SURVIVE IT?

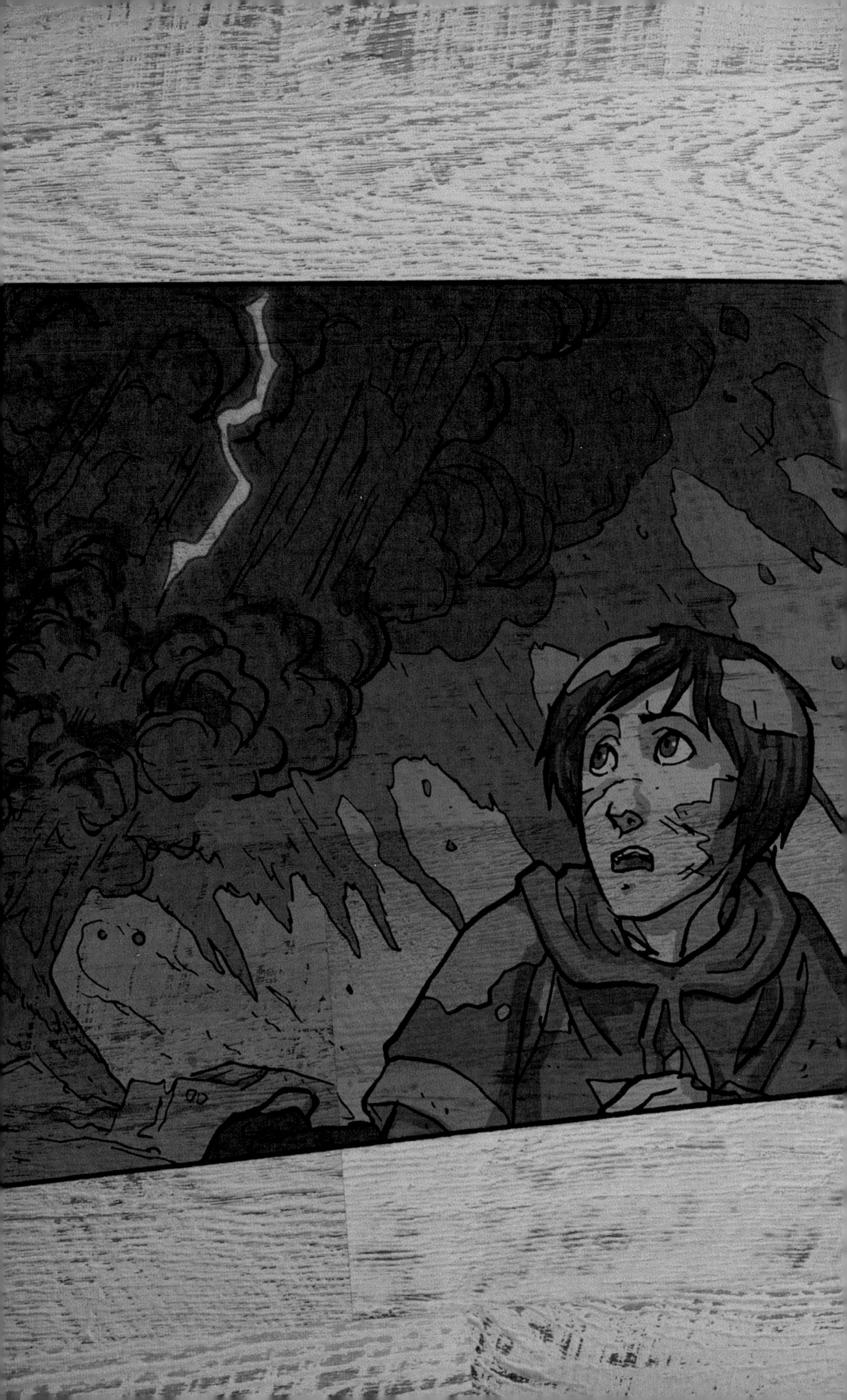

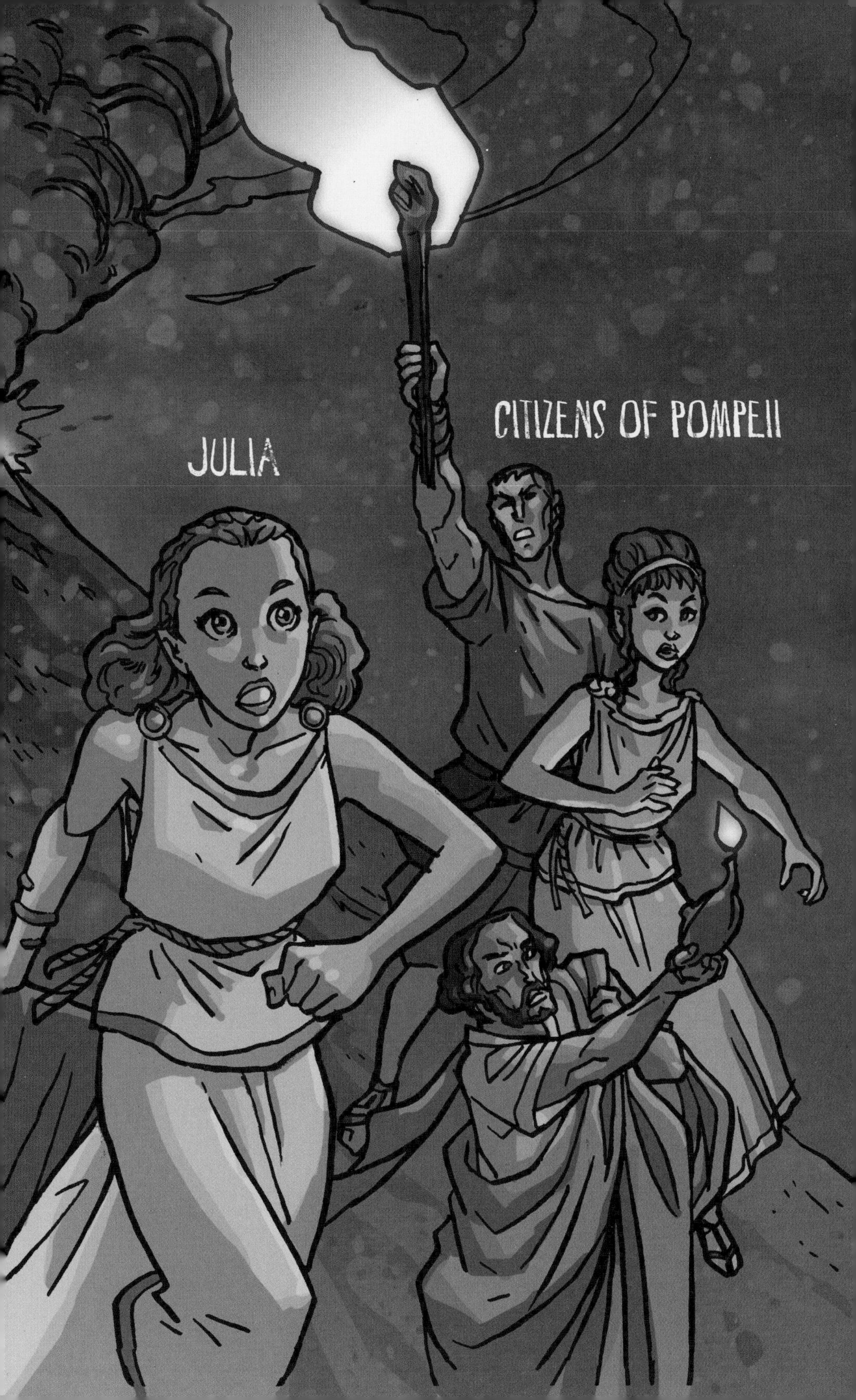
CITIZENS OF POMPEII
JULIA

CHAPTER ONE
MOVING DAY

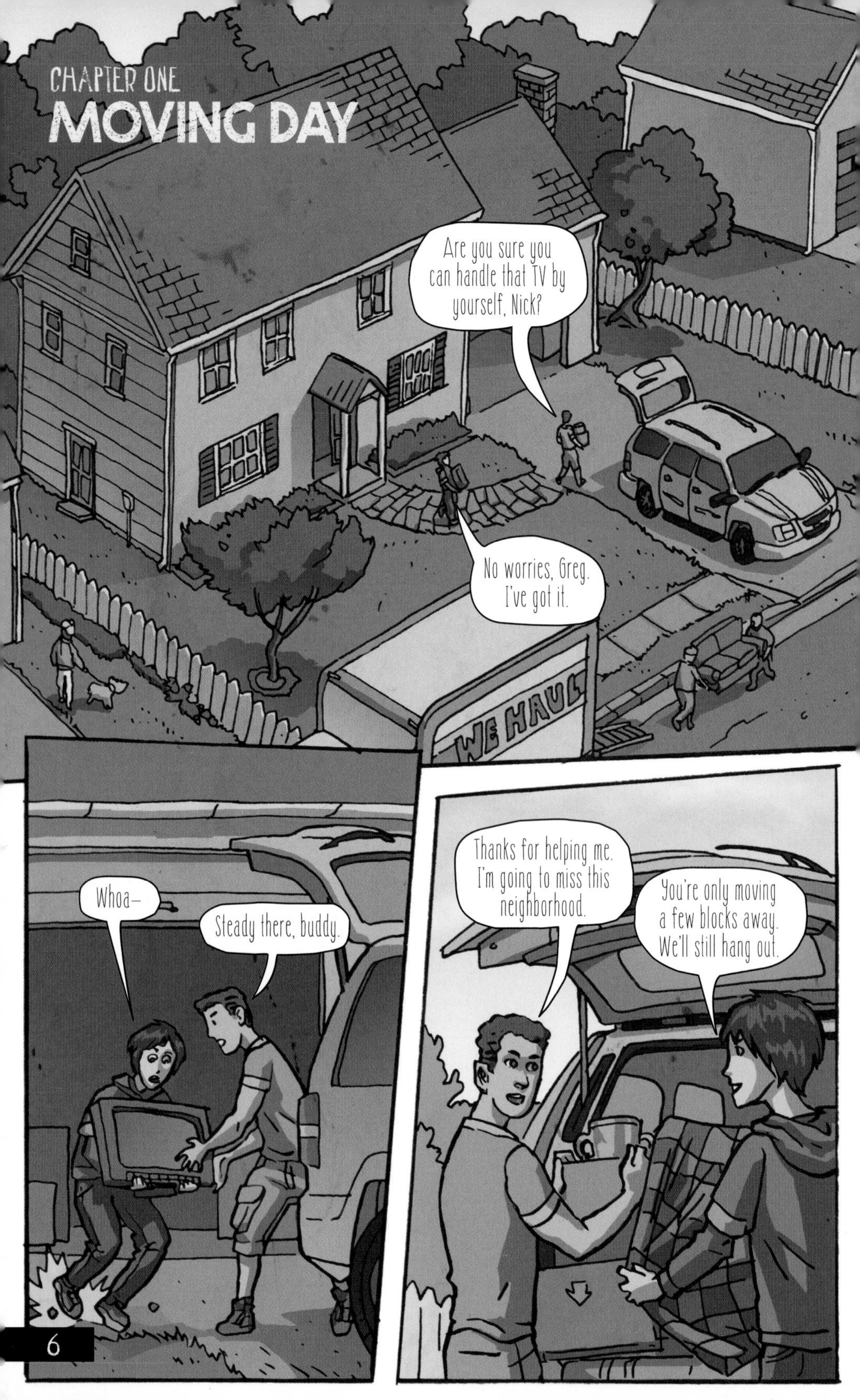
Are you sure you can handle that TV by yourself, Nick?
No worries, Greg. I've got it.
WE HAUL
Whoa—
Steady there, buddy.
Thanks for helping me. I'm going to miss this neighborhood.
You're only moving a few blocks away. We'll still hang out.

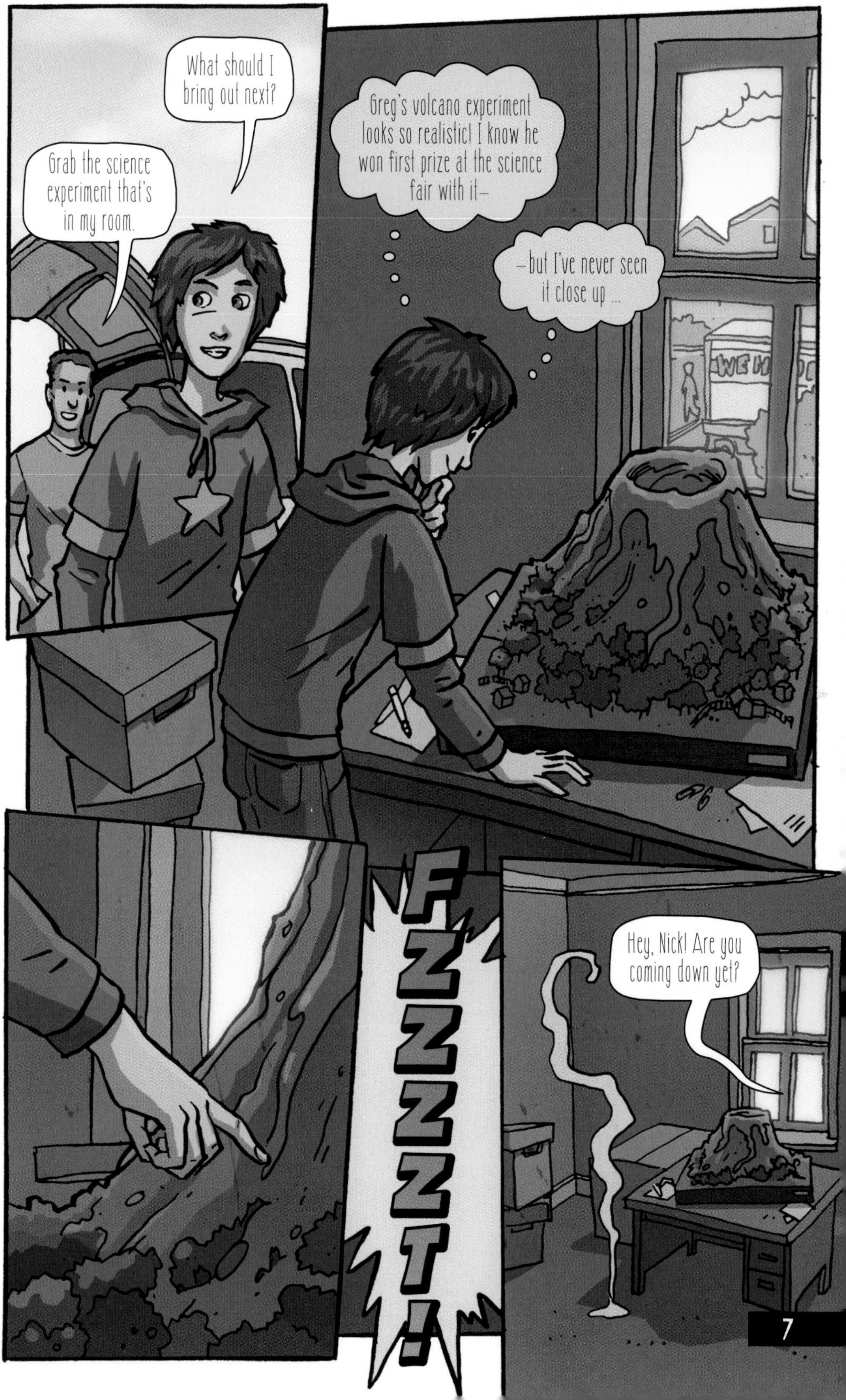

What should I bring out next?
Grab the science experiment that's in my room.
Greg's volcano experiment looks so realistic! I know he won first prize at the science fair with it–
–but I've never seen it close up ...
FZZZZT!
Hey, Nick! Are you coming down yet?

CHAPTER TWO
THE GREAT ESCAPE

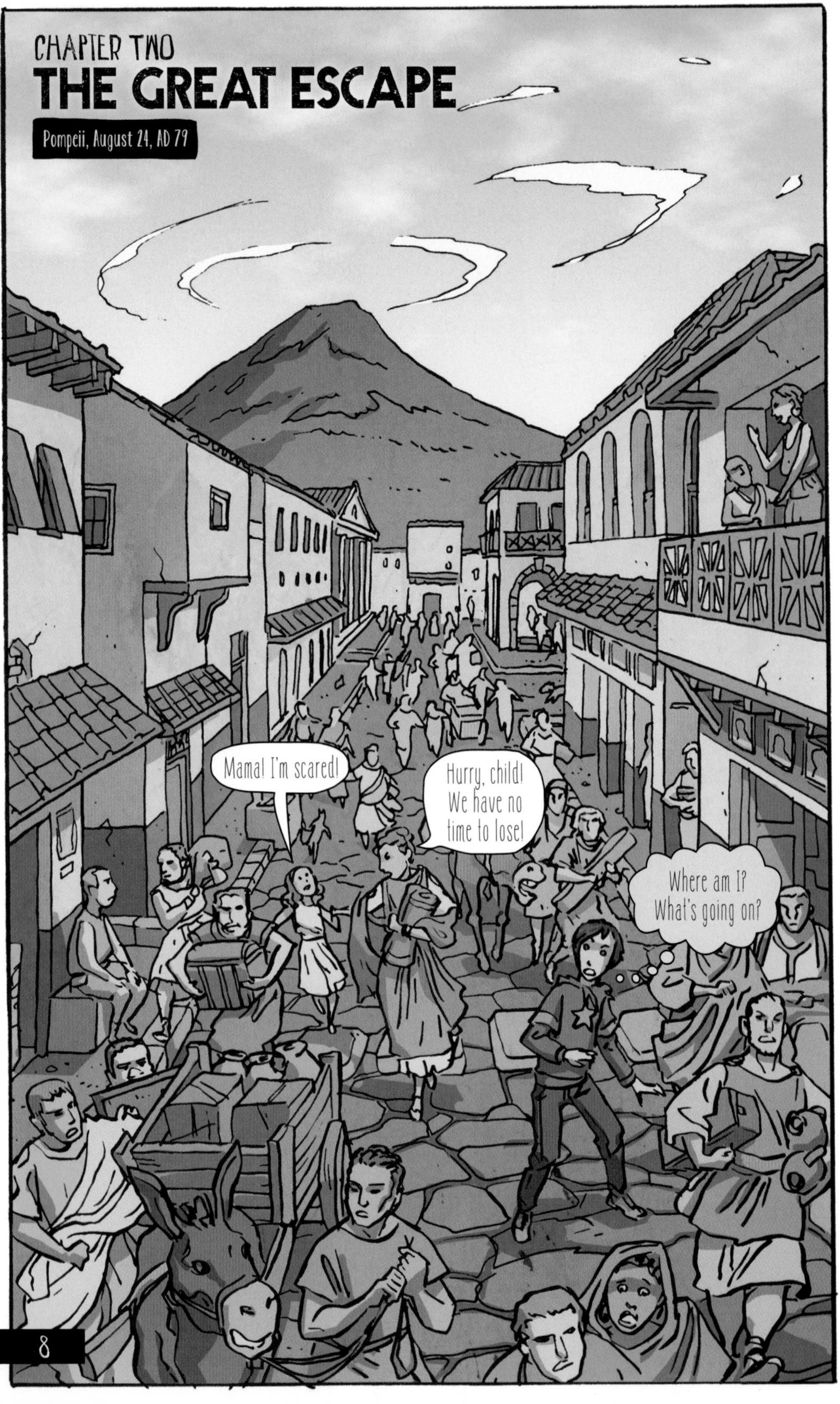
Pompeii, August 24, AD 79
Mama! I'm scared!
Hurry, child! We have no time to lose!
Where am I? What's going on?

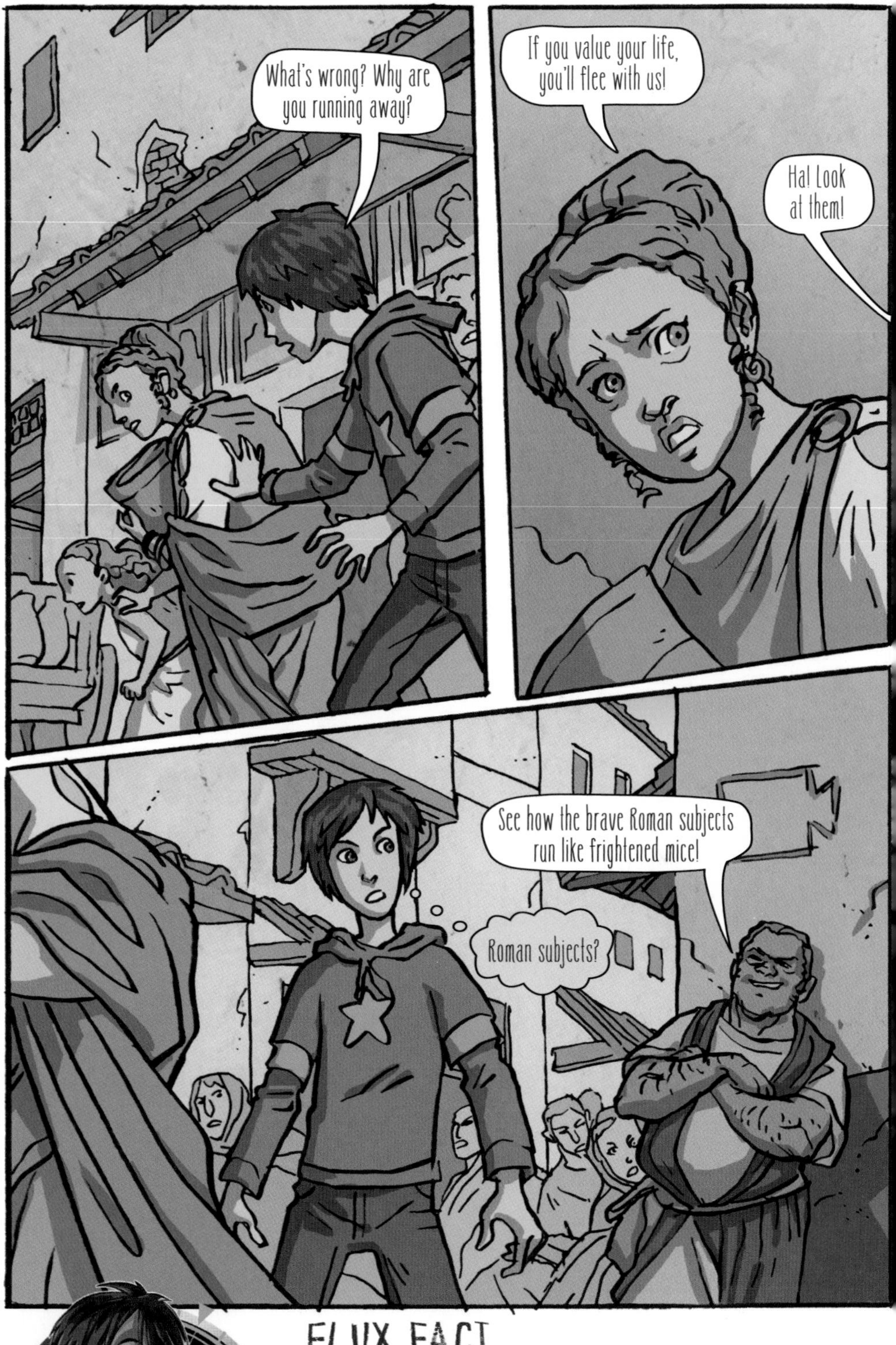
What's wrong? Why are you running away?
If you value your life, you'll flee with us!
Ha! Look at them!
See how the brave Roman subjects run like frightened mice!
Roman subjects?

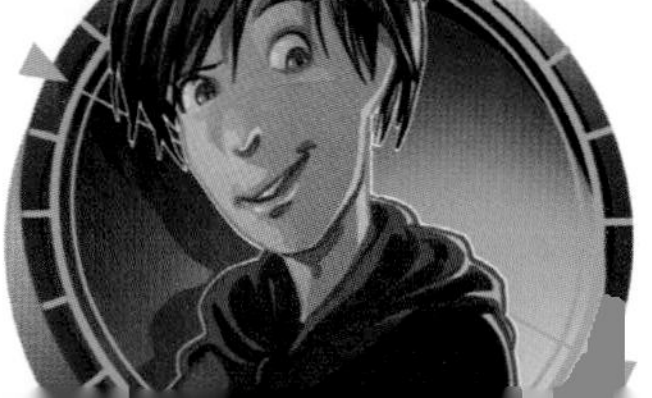

FLUX FACT

Mount Vesuvius and the ancient city of Pompeii lie on the western coast of modern-day Italy, about 7 miles (11 kilometers) apart. In ancient times Pompeii was an important and wealthy commercial center.

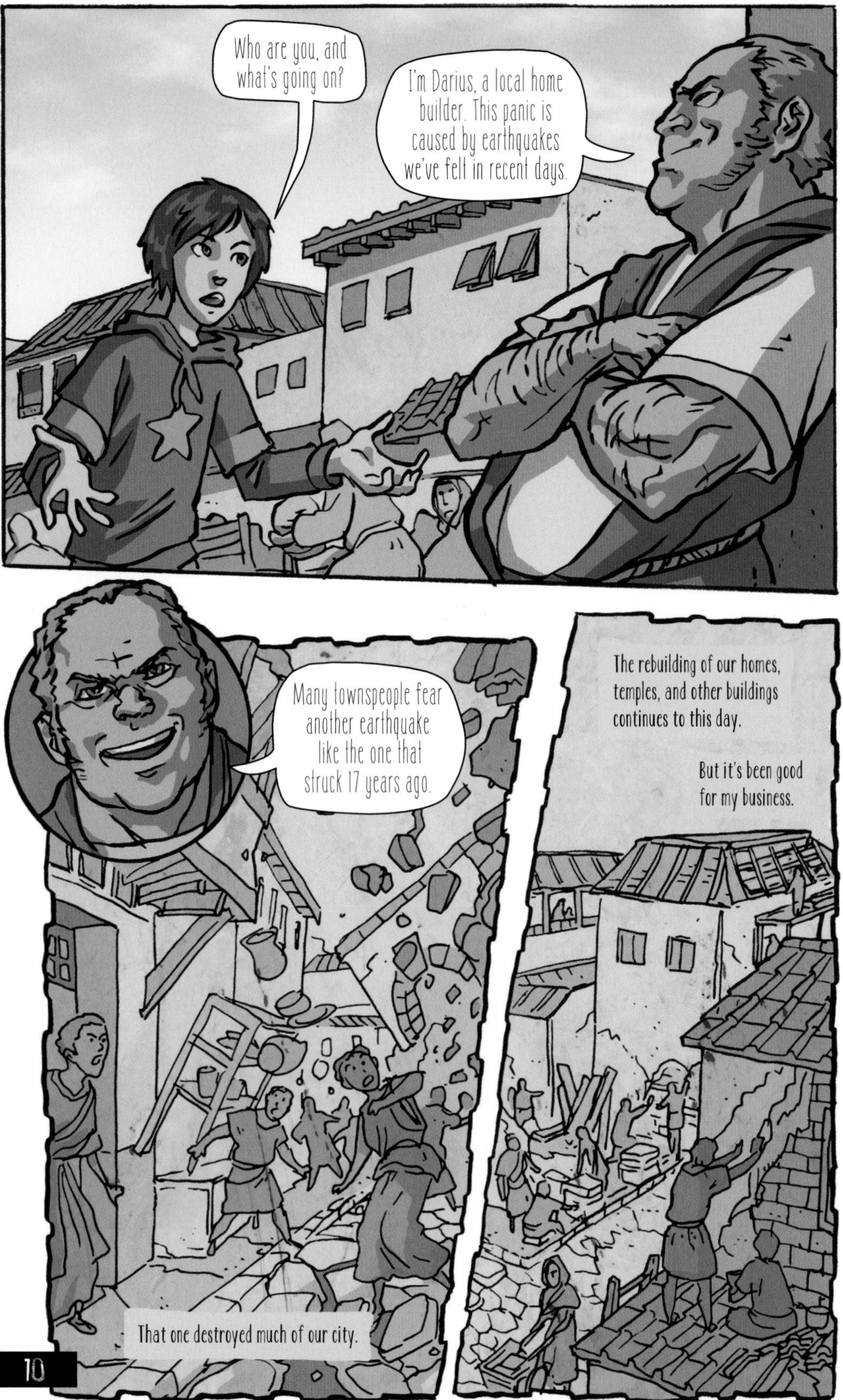
Who are you, and what's going on?
I'm Darius, a local home builder. This panic is caused by earthquakes we've felt in recent days.
Many townspeople fear another earthquake like the one that struck 17 years ago.
That one destroyed much of our city.
The rebuilding of our homes, temples, and other buildings continues to this day.
But it's been good for my business.

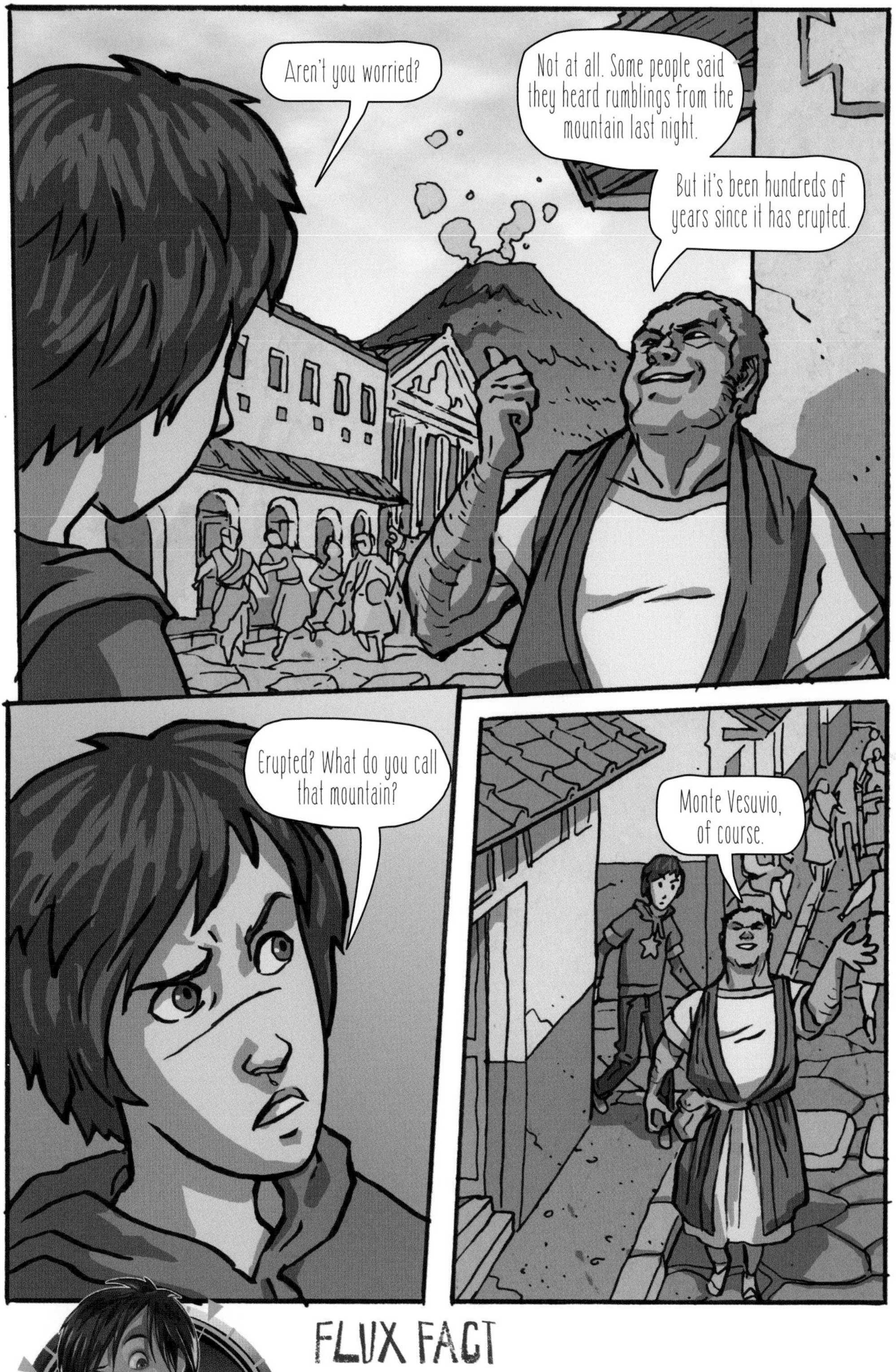
Aren't you worried?
Not at all. Some people said they heard rumblings from the mountain last night.
But it's been hundreds of years since it has erupted.
Erupted? What do you call that mountain?
Monte Vesuvio, of course.

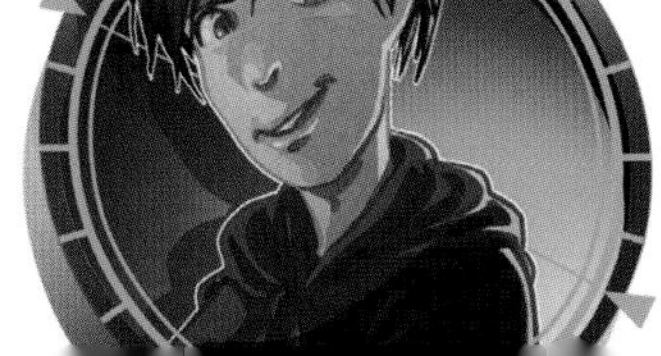

FLUX FACT

The earthquake in AD 62 did more than damage buildings. It caused cracks in the Earth's crust that released poisonous gas. One Roman writer reported that 600 sheep were killed by "tainted air."

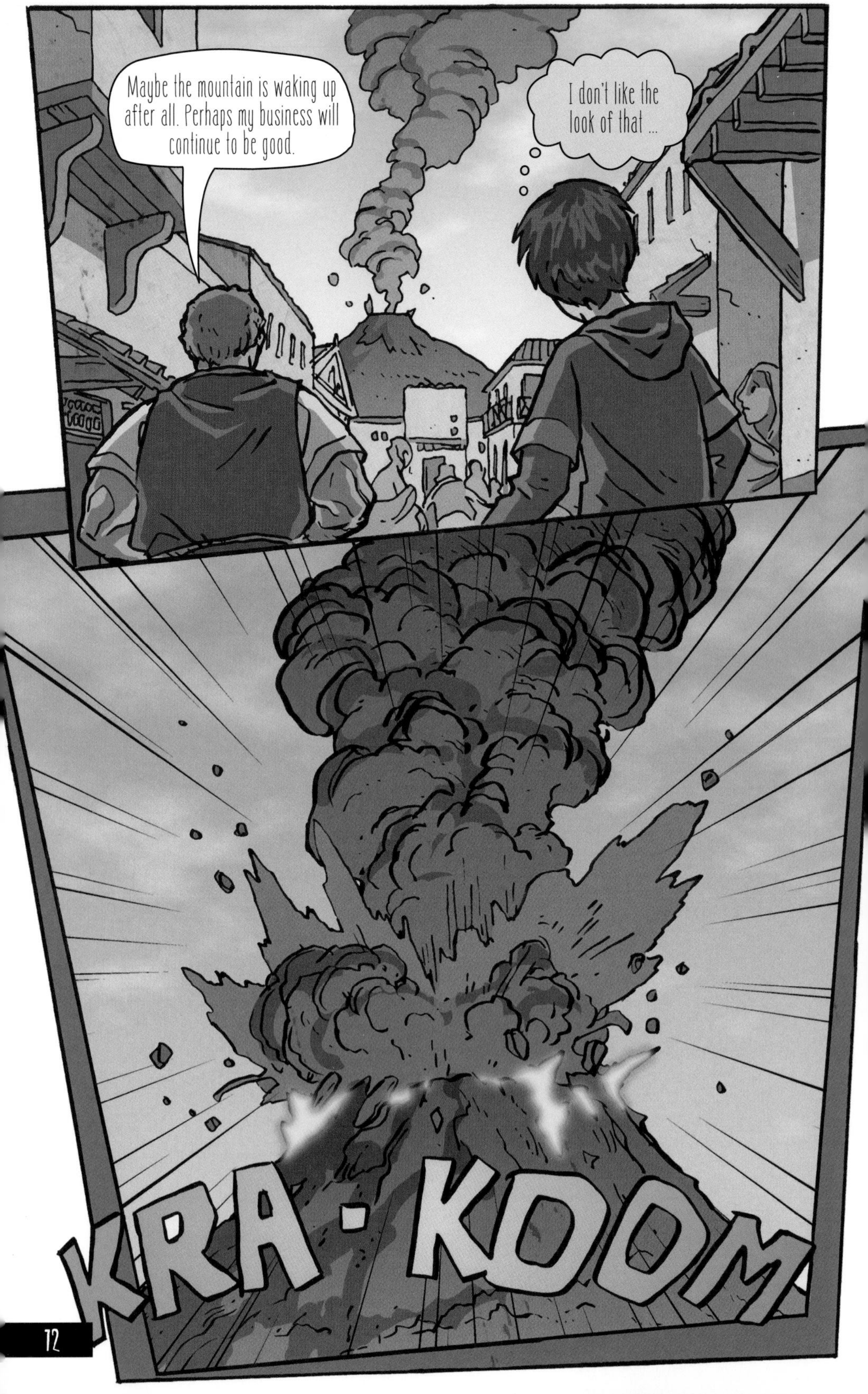
Maybe the mountain is waking up after all. Perhaps my business will continue to be good.
I don't like the look of that ...
KRA-KOOM

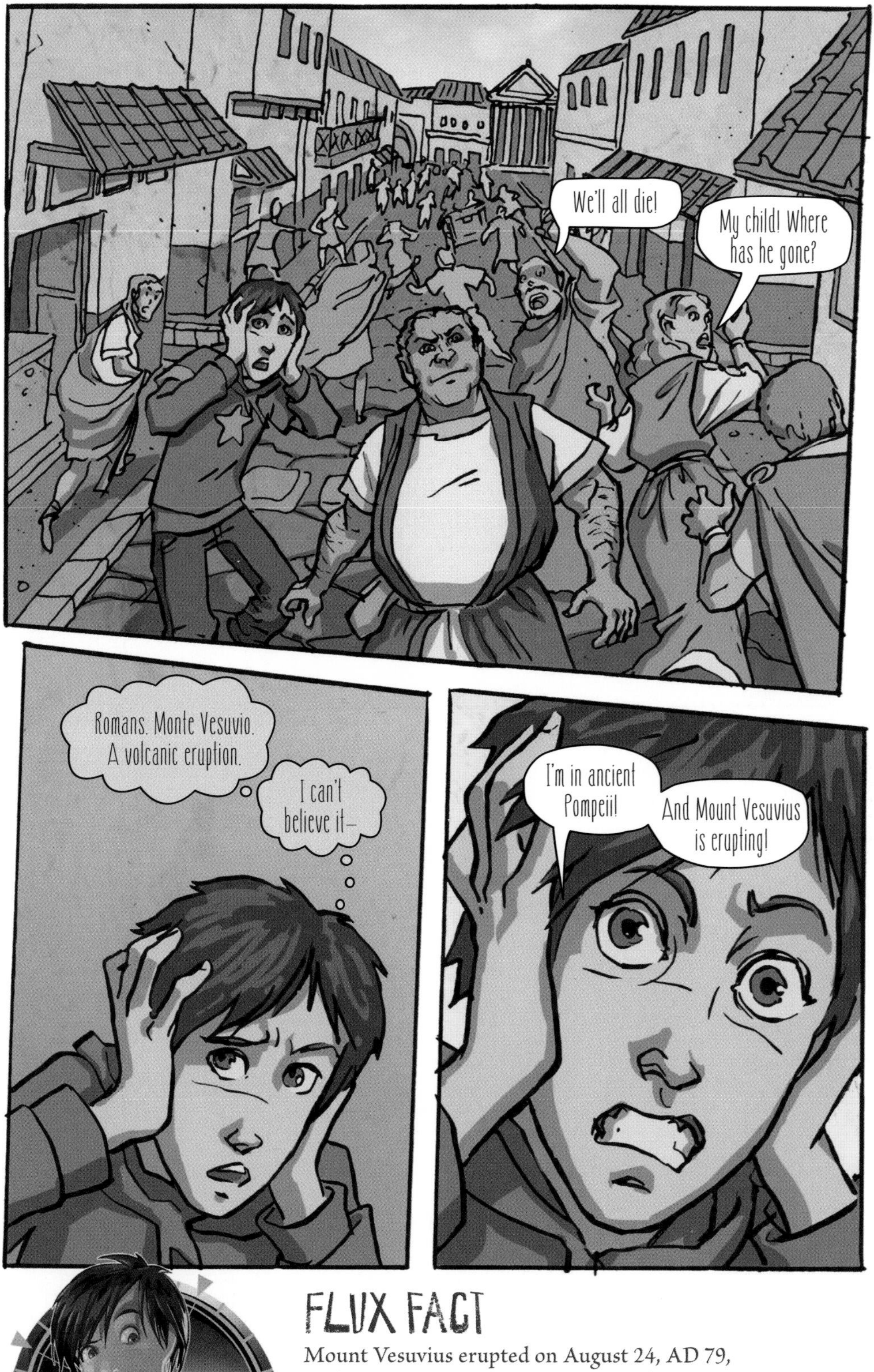
We'll all die!
My child! Where has he gone?
Romans. Monte Vesuvio. A volcanic eruption.
I can't believe it—
I'm in ancient Pompeii!
And Mount Vesuvius is erupting!

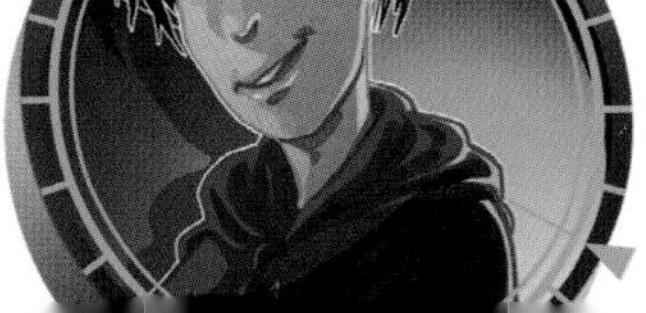

FLUX FACT

Mount Vesuvius erupted on August 24, AD 79, at about 1:00 p.m. The eruption lasted 18 hours. Vesuvius has erupted about 100 times since then, and it is still an active volcano.

CHAPTER THREE
FURY OF VESUVIUS

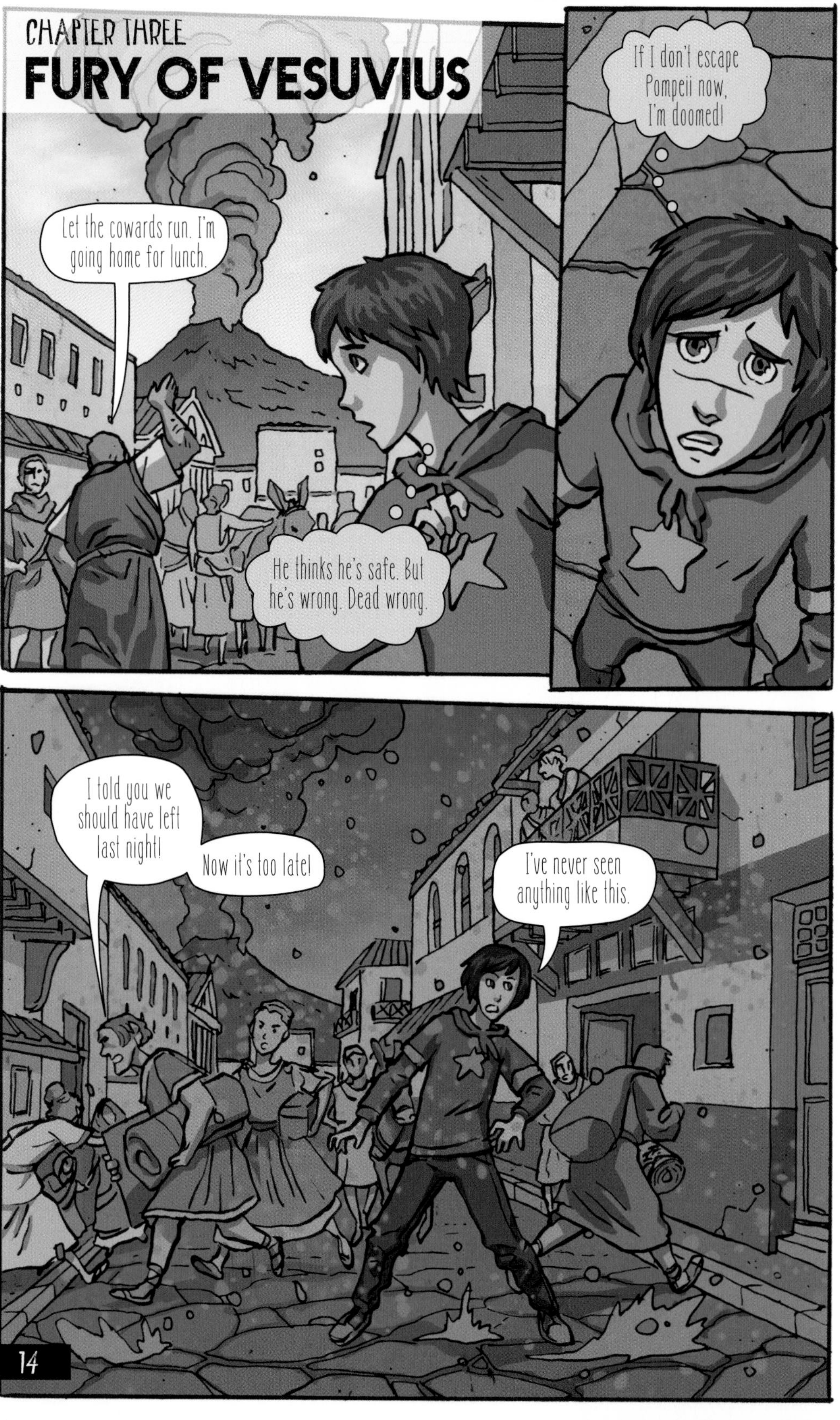
Let the cowards run. I'm going home for lunch.
He thinks he's safe. But he's wrong. Dead wrong.
If I don't escape Pompeii now, I'm doomed!
I told you we should have left last night!
Now it's too late!
I've never seen anything like this.

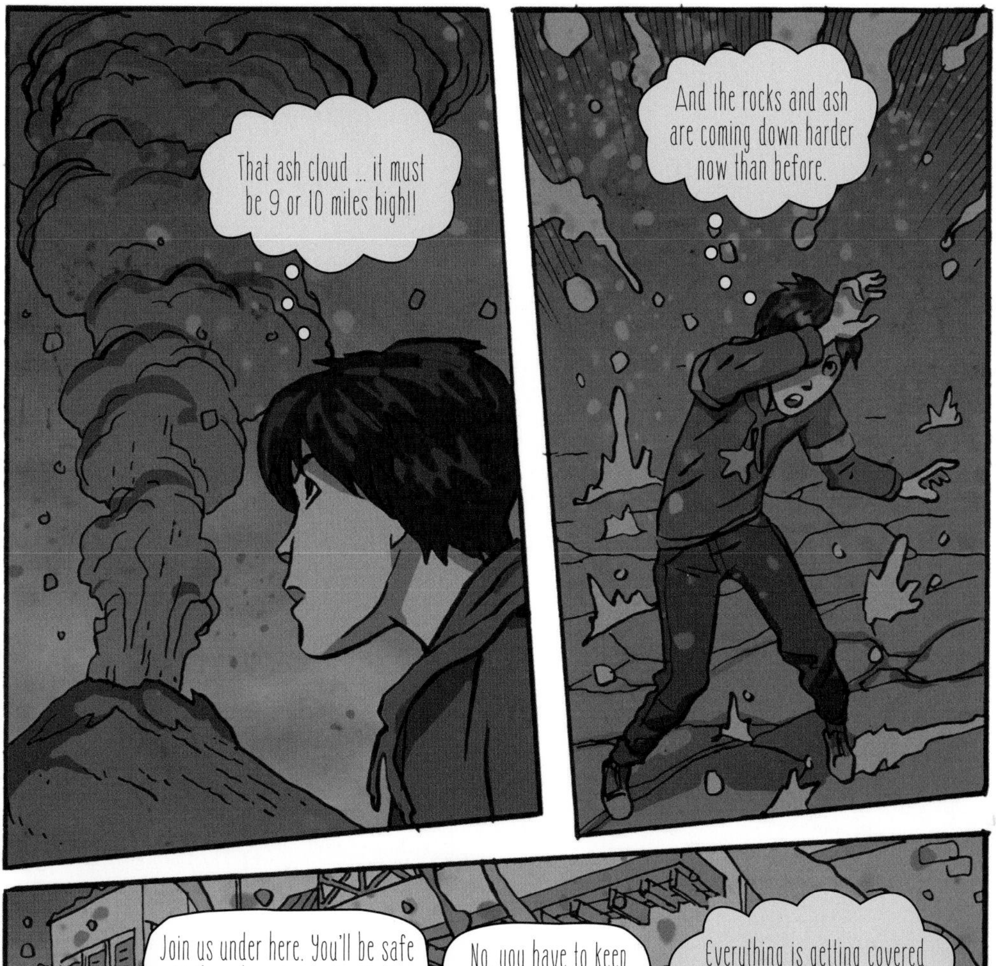
That ash cloud ... it must be 9 or 10 miles high!!
And the rocks and ash are coming down harder now than before.
Join us under here. You'll be safe until the ash and rock stop falling.
No, you have to keep moving! Nowhere in this city is safe.
Everything is getting covered with the fallout, especially these wooden rooftops.

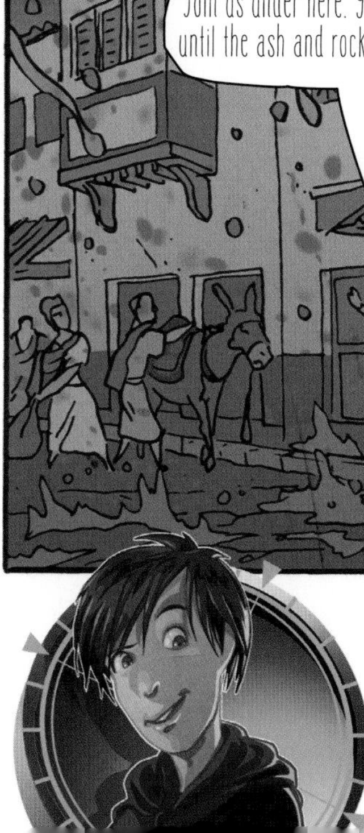

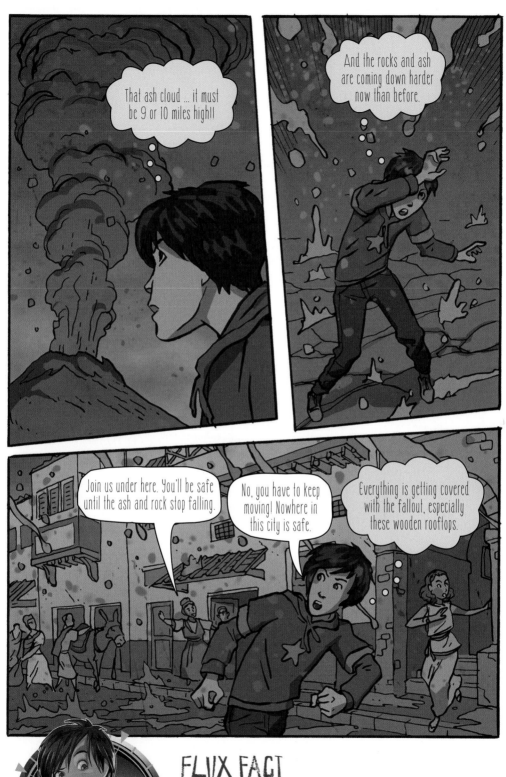

FLUX FACT

No one knows for certain how many people lived in Pompeii at the time of the AD 79 eruption. Estimates range from 6,400 to 30,000 inhabitants.

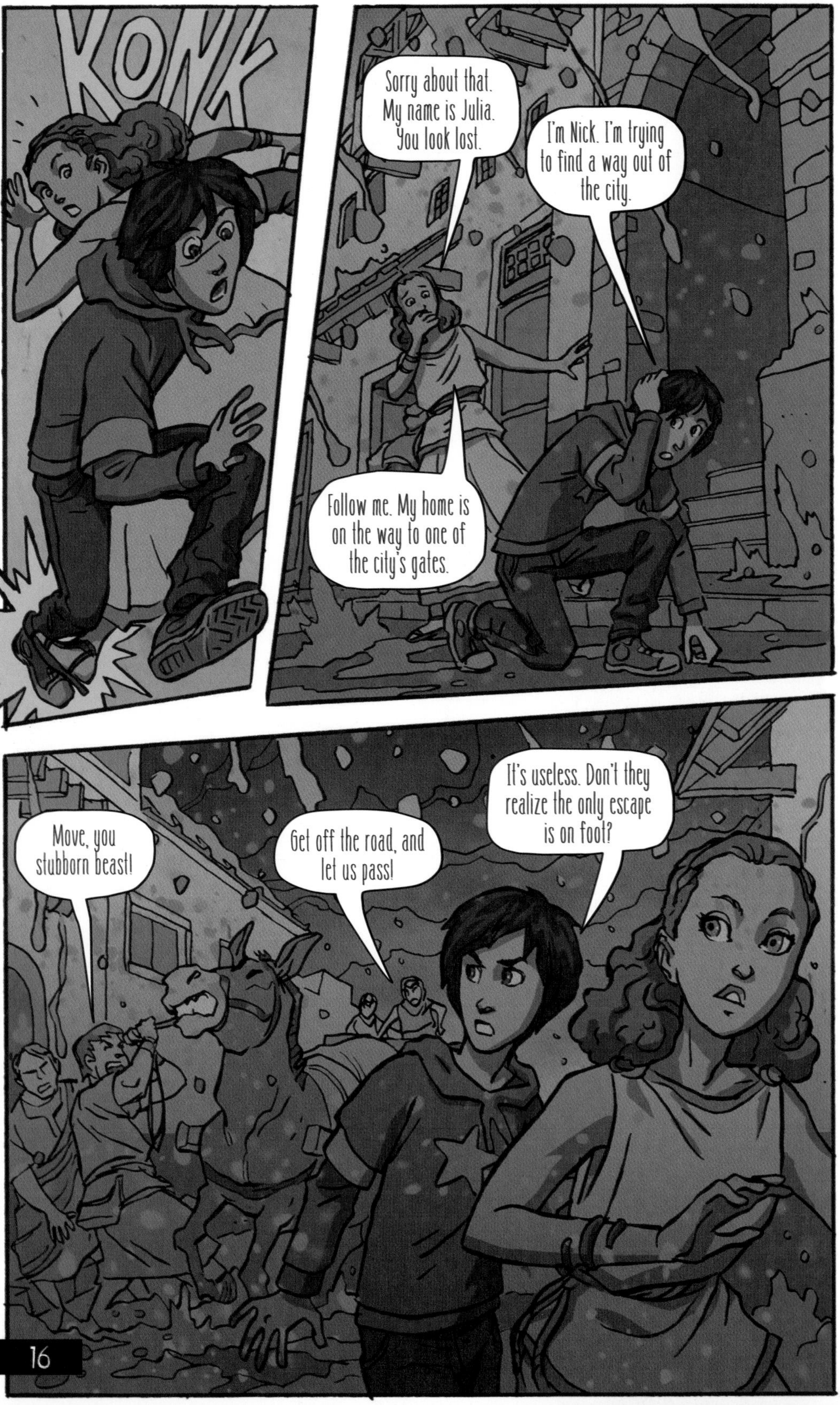
KONK
Sorry about that. My name is Julia. You look lost.
I'm Nick. I'm trying to find a way out of the city.
Follow me. My home is on the way to one of the city's gates.
Move, you stubborn beast!
Get off the road, and let us pass!
It's useless. Don't they realize the only escape is on foot?

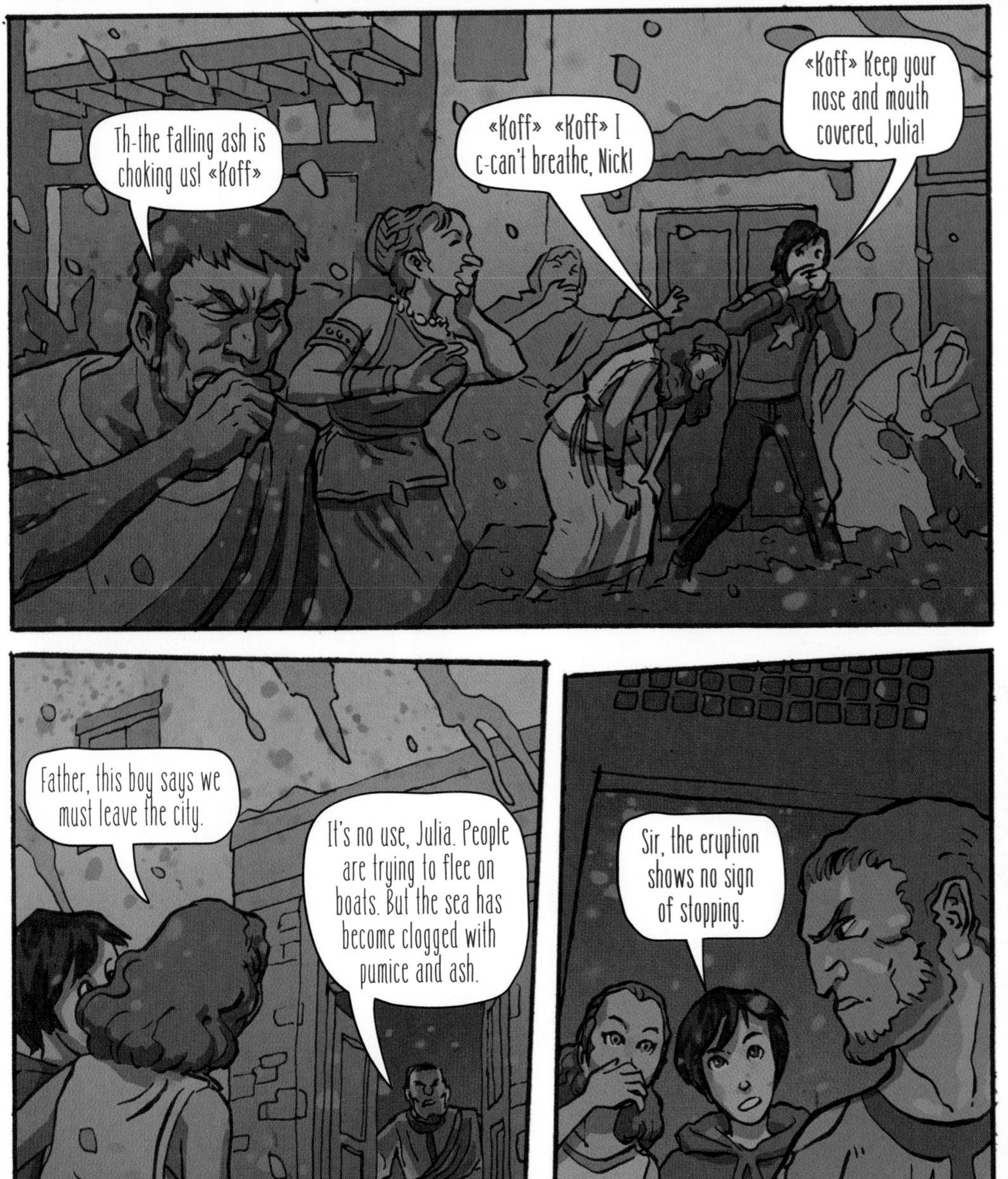
Th-the falling ash is choking us! «Koff»
«Koff» «Koff» I c-can't breathe, Nick!
«Koff» Keep your nose and mouth covered, Julia!
Father, this boy says we must leave the city.
It's no use, Julia. People are trying to flee on boats. But the sea has become clogged with pumice and ash.
Sir, the eruption shows no sign of stopping.
Then we'll stay indoors where it's safer. Come inside, quickly.

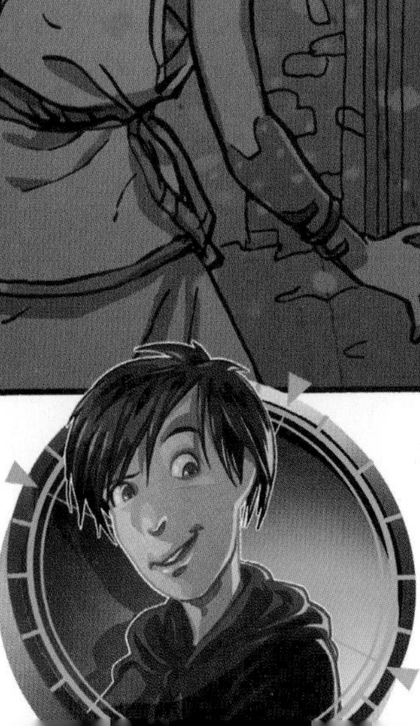

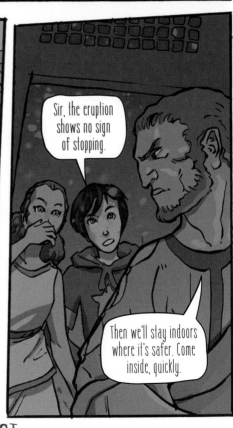

FLUX FACT

Pumice forms during volcanic eruptions when lava containing gas bubbles is shot into the air. As the lava hardens, the bubbles become part of the rock. Pumice is so lightweight that it floats on water.

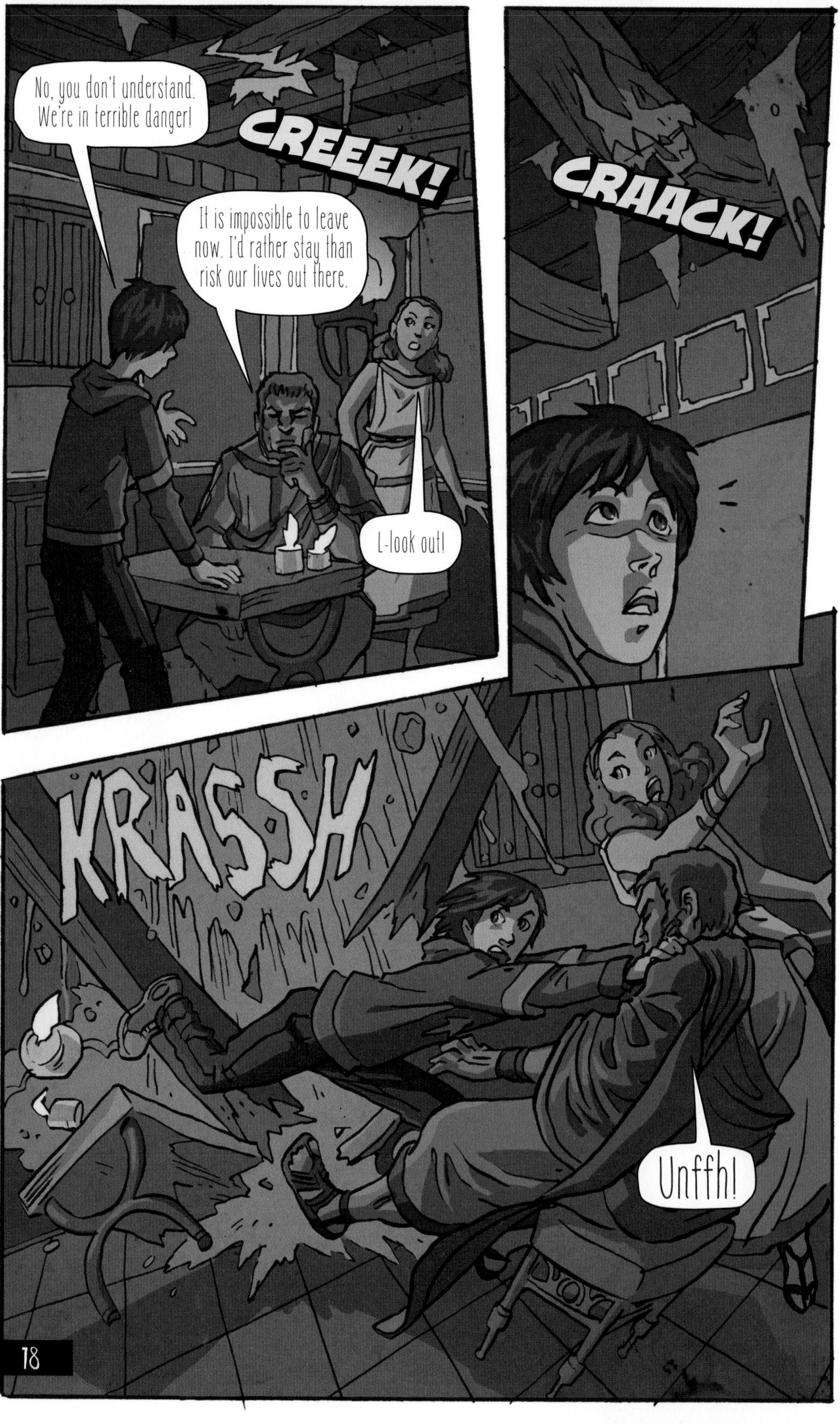

No, you don't understand. We're in terrible danger!
CREEEK!
It is impossible to leave now. I'd rather stay than risk our lives out there.
L-look out!
CRAACK!
KRASSH
Unffh!

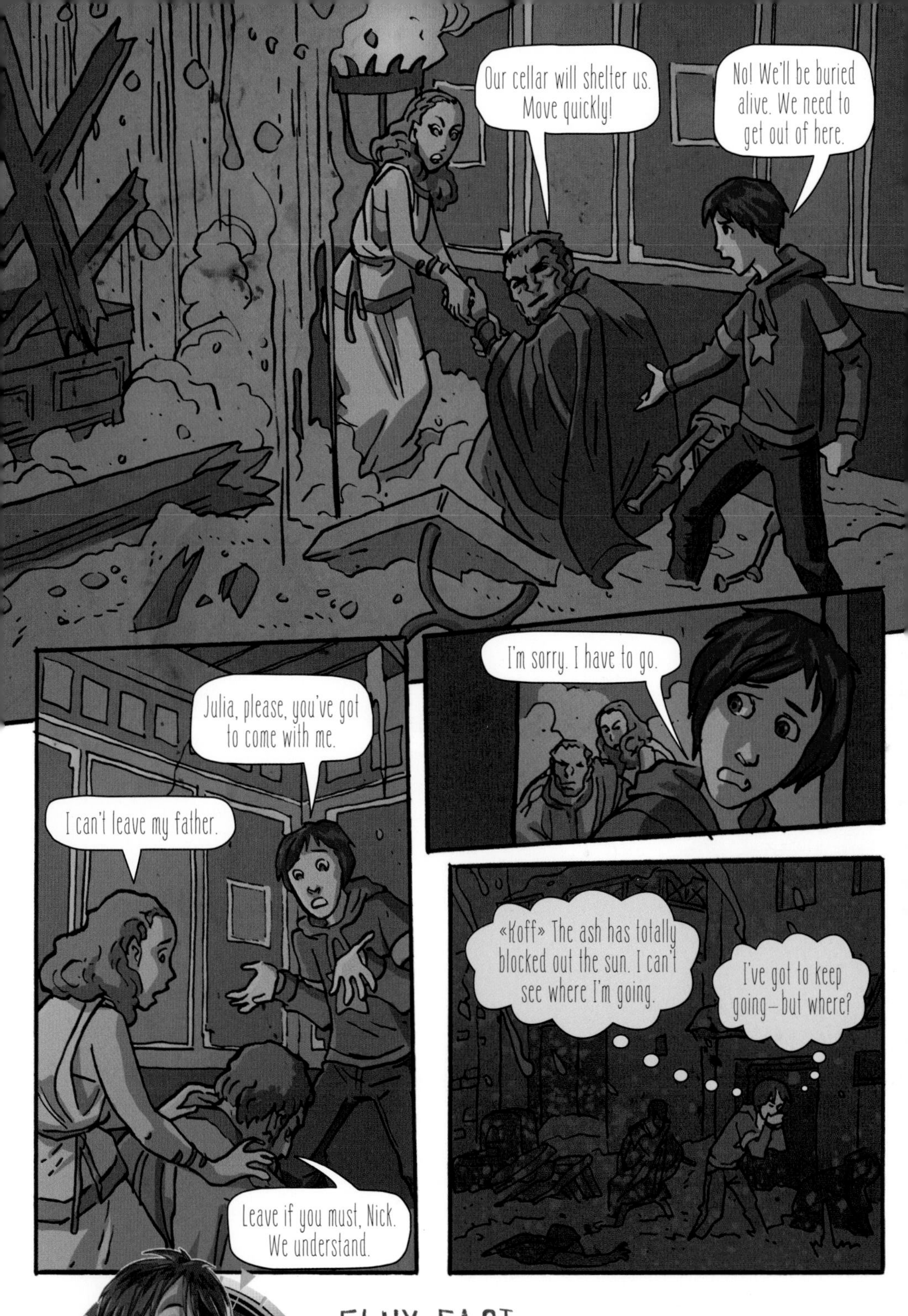
Our cellar will shelter us. Move quickly!
No! We'll be buried alive. We need to get out of here.
Julia, please, you've got to come with me.
I can't leave my father.
Leave if you must, Nick. We understand.
I'm sorry. I have to go.
«Koff» The ash has totally blocked out the sun. I can't see where I'm going.
I've got to keep going—but where?

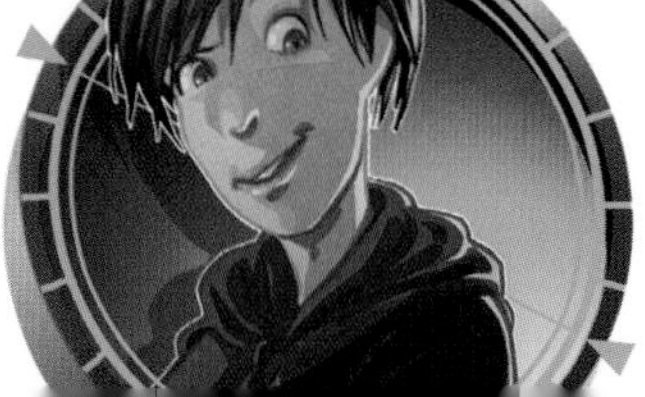

FLUX FACT

Pompeii was buried in 25 feet (7.6 meters) of ash. For months after the eruption, thieves tunneled through the ash to find buried valuables in the city.

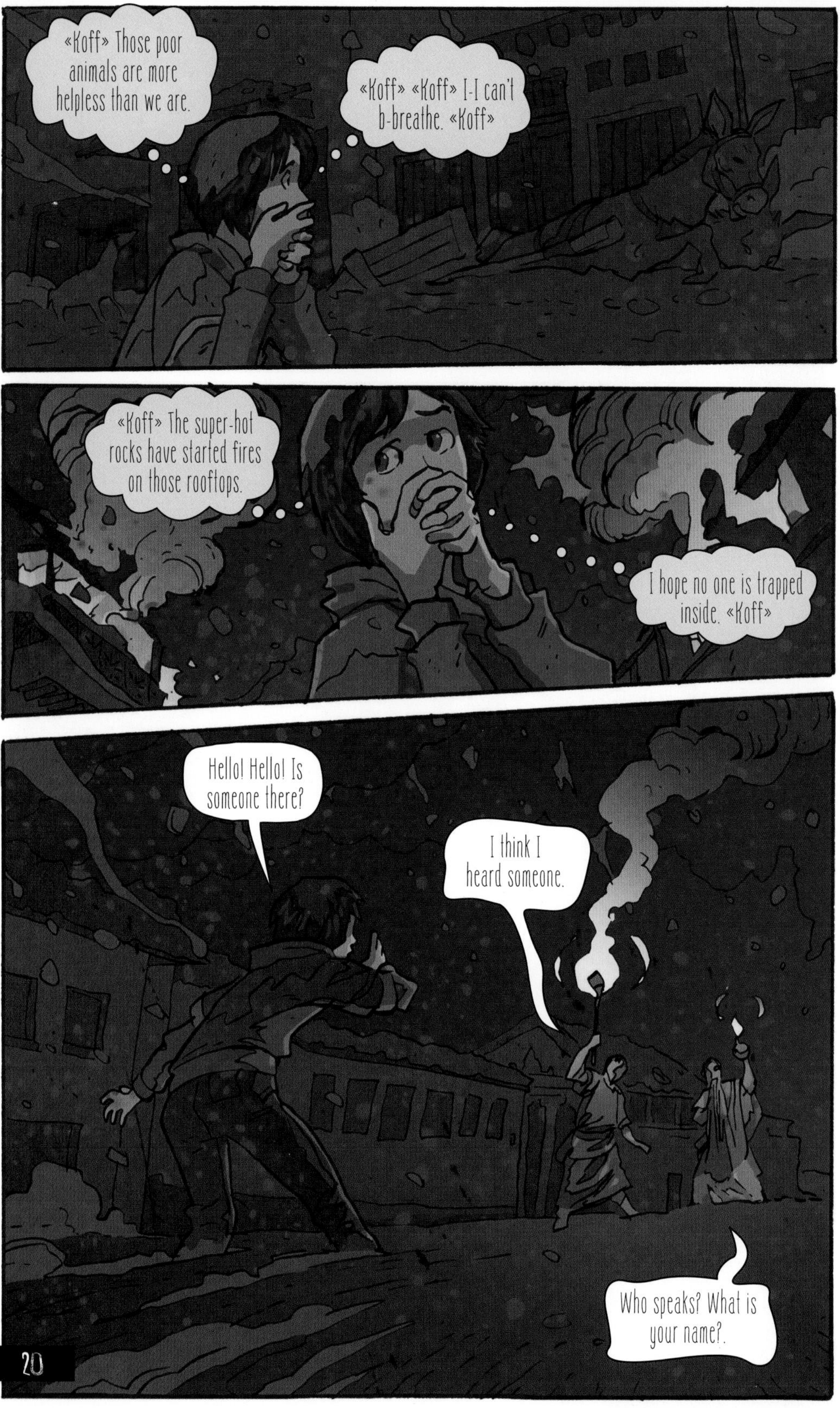
«Koff» Those poor animals are more helpless than we are.
«Koff» «Koff» I-I can't b-breathe. «Koff»
«Koff» The super-hot rocks have started fires on those rooftops.
I hope no one is trapped inside. «Koff»
Hello! Hello! Is someone there?
I think I heard someone.
Who speaks? What is your name?.

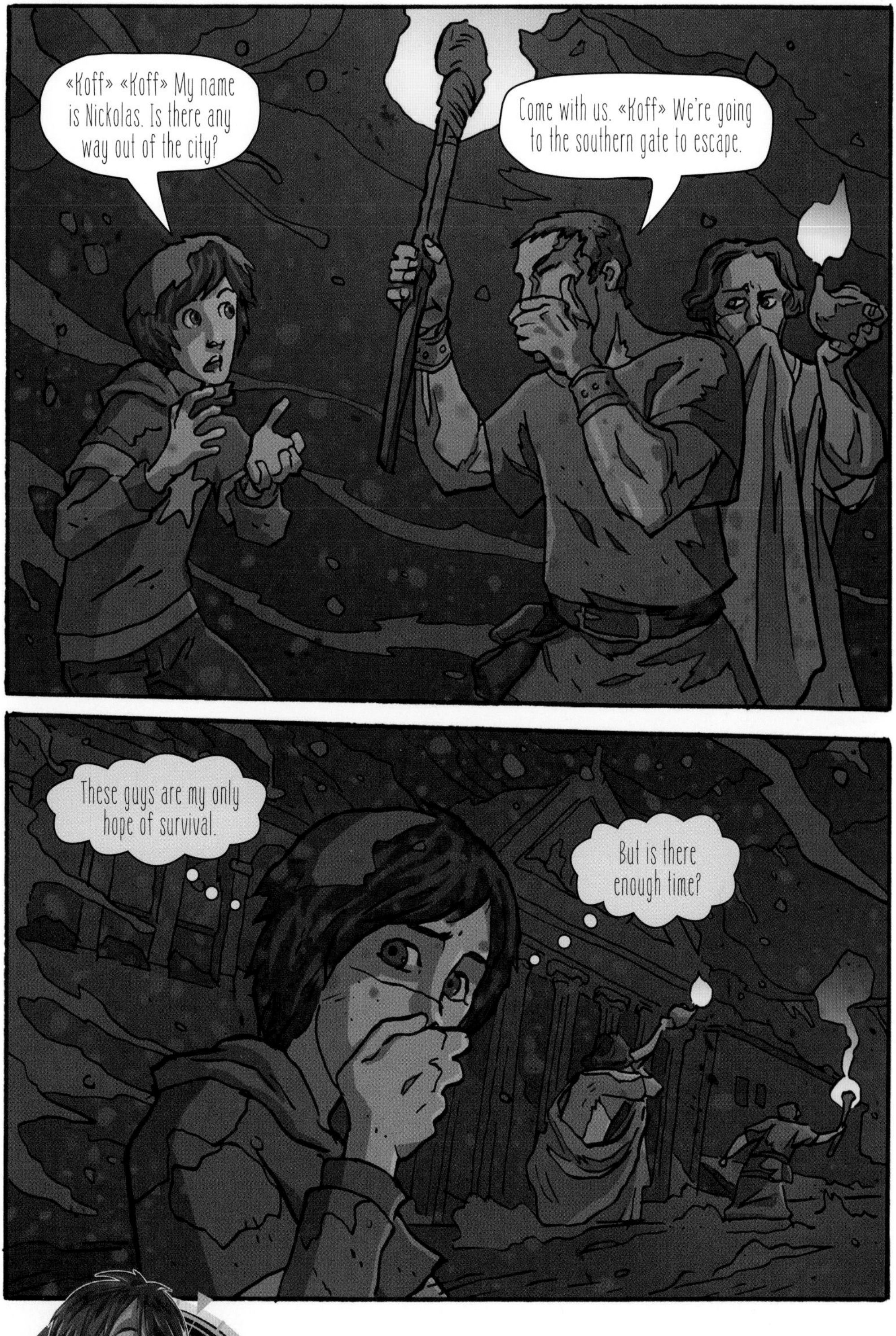
«Koff» «Koff» My name is Nickolas. Is there any way out of the city?
Come with us. «Koff» We're going to the southern gate to escape.
These guys are my only hope of survival.
But is there enough time?

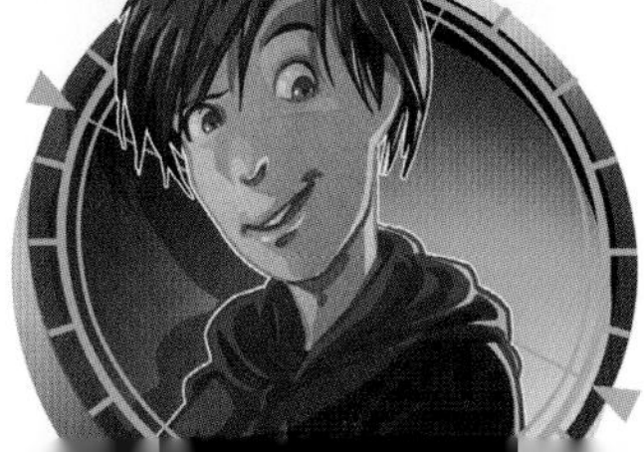

FLUX FACT

An area of roughly 115 square miles (300 sq km) was burned around Pompeii. Not a living thing remained in that area. Ash fell as far away as North Africa.

CHAPTER FOUR

MORNING OF DOOM

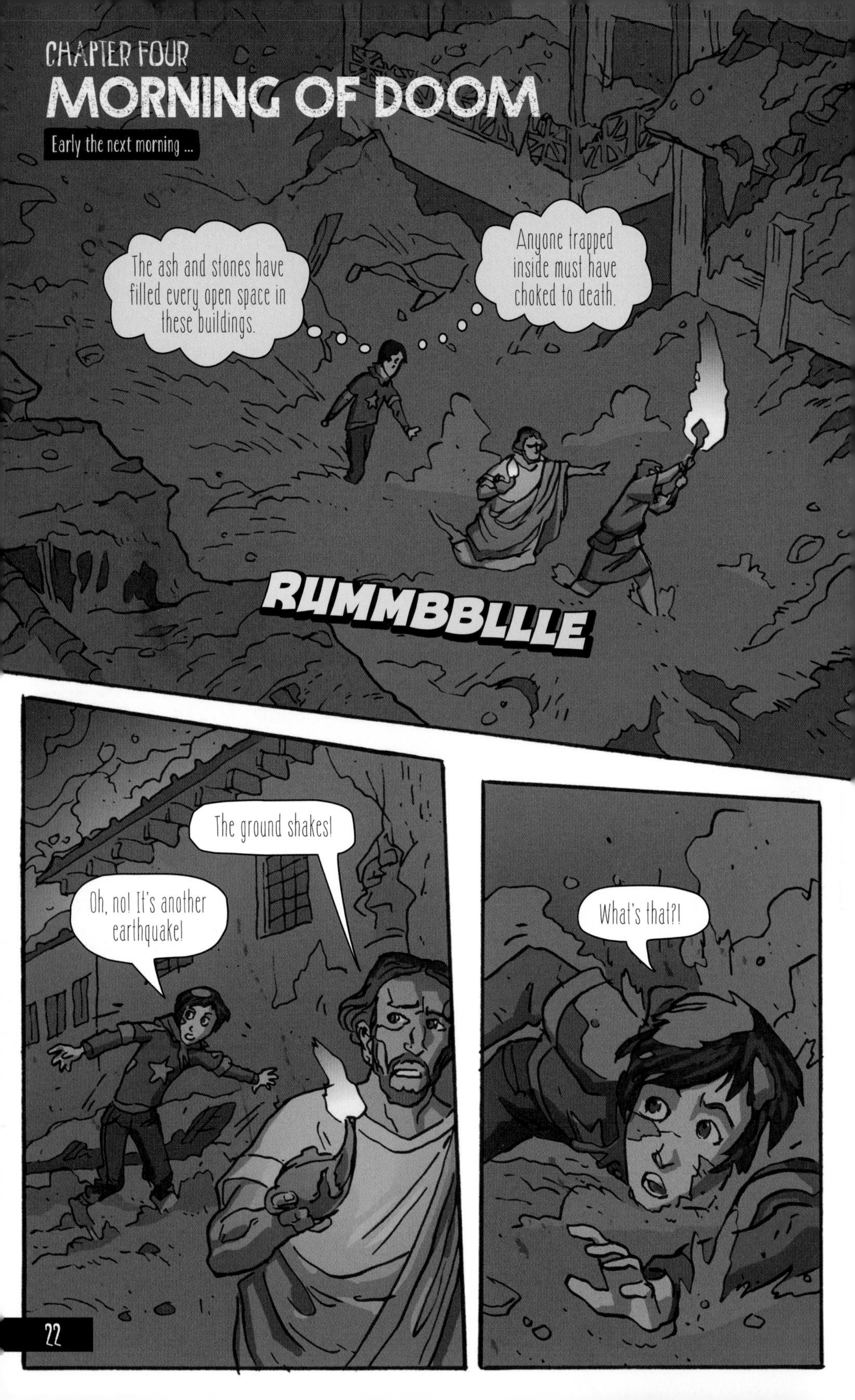
Early the next morning ...
The ash and stones have filled every open space in these buildings.
Anyone trapped inside must have choked to death.
RUMMBBLLLE
The ground shakes!
Oh, no! It's another earthquake!
What's that?!

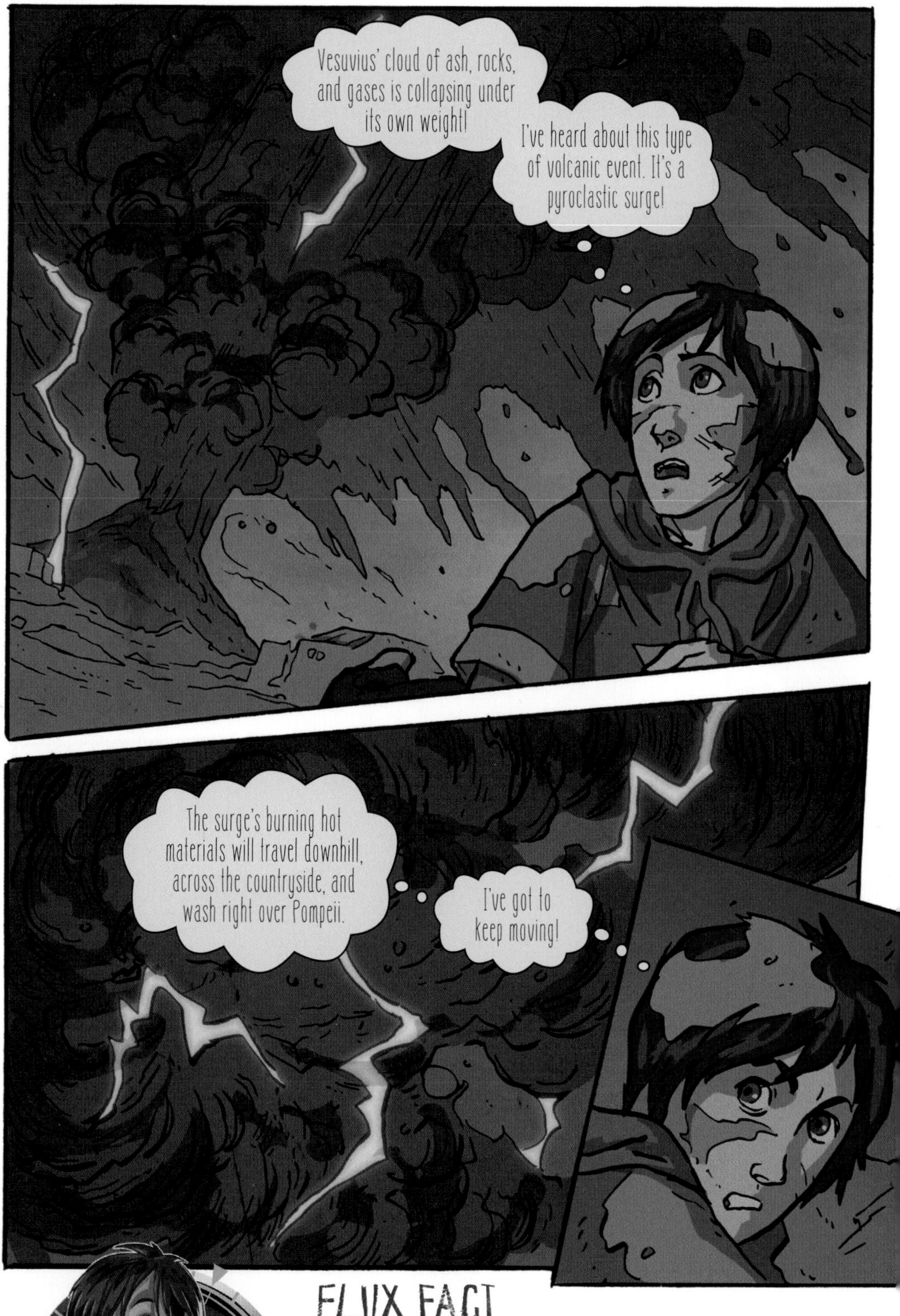

Vesuvius' cloud of ash, rocks, and gases is collapsing under its own weight!
I've heard about this type of volcanic event. It's a pyroclastic surge!
The surge's burning hot materials will travel downhill, across the countryside, and wash right over Pompeii.
I've got to keep moving!

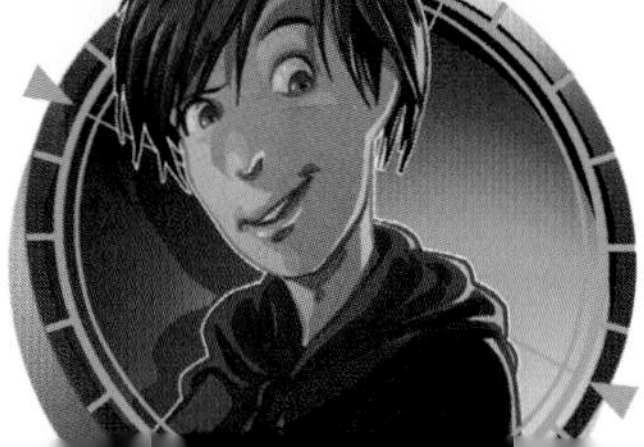

FLUX FACT

Pyroclastic surges can top speeds of 300 miles (480 km) per hour. They contain a deadly mixture of gas, ash, and steam. The temperature of a surge can reach 1,500° Fahrenheit (815° Celsius).

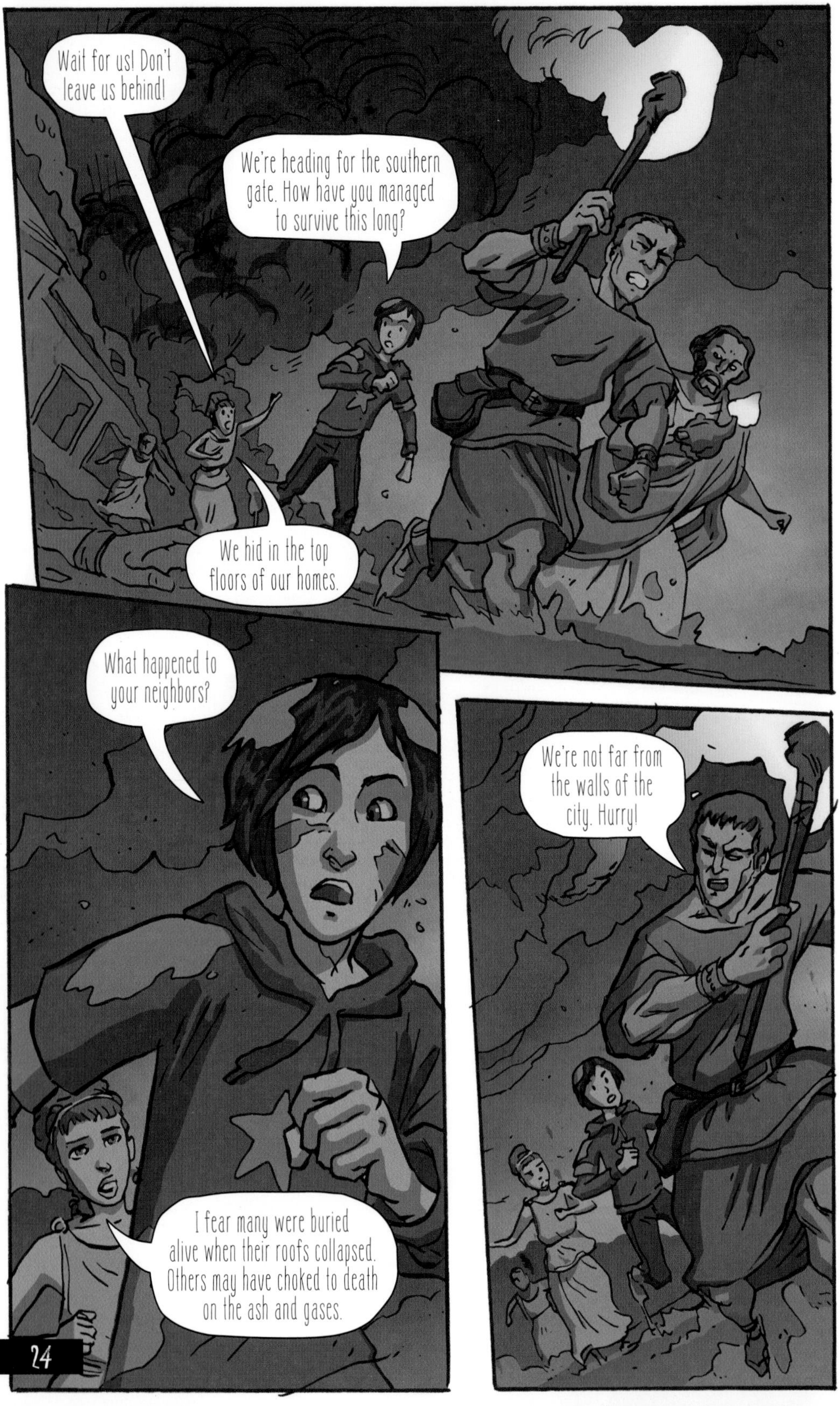
Wait for us! Don't leave us behind!
We're heading for the southern gate. How have you managed to survive this long?
We hid in the top floors of our homes.
What happened to your neighbors?
I fear many were buried alive when their roofs collapsed. Others may have choked to death on the ash and gases.
We're not far from the walls of the city. Hurry!

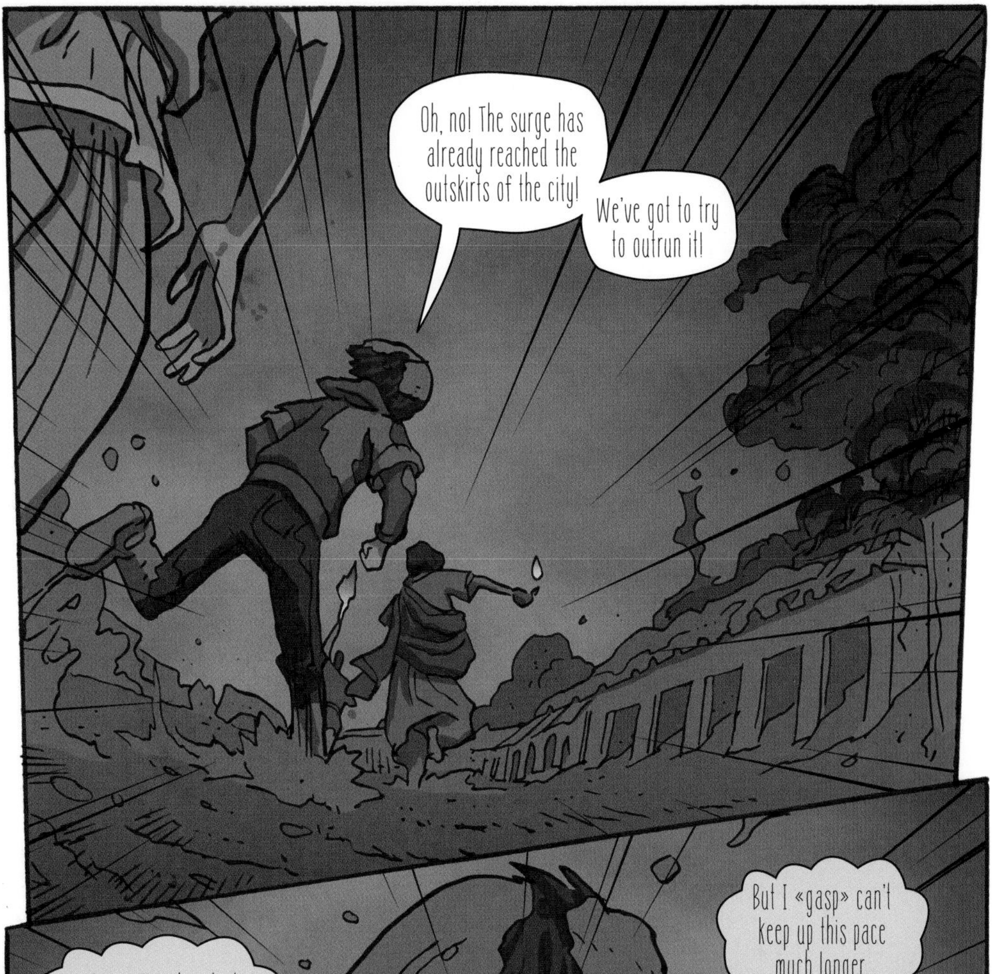
Oh, no! The surge has already reached the outskirts of the city!
We've got to try to outrun it!
«Gasp» I'm almost at the city gate! «Gasp»
But I «gasp» can't keep up this pace much longer.

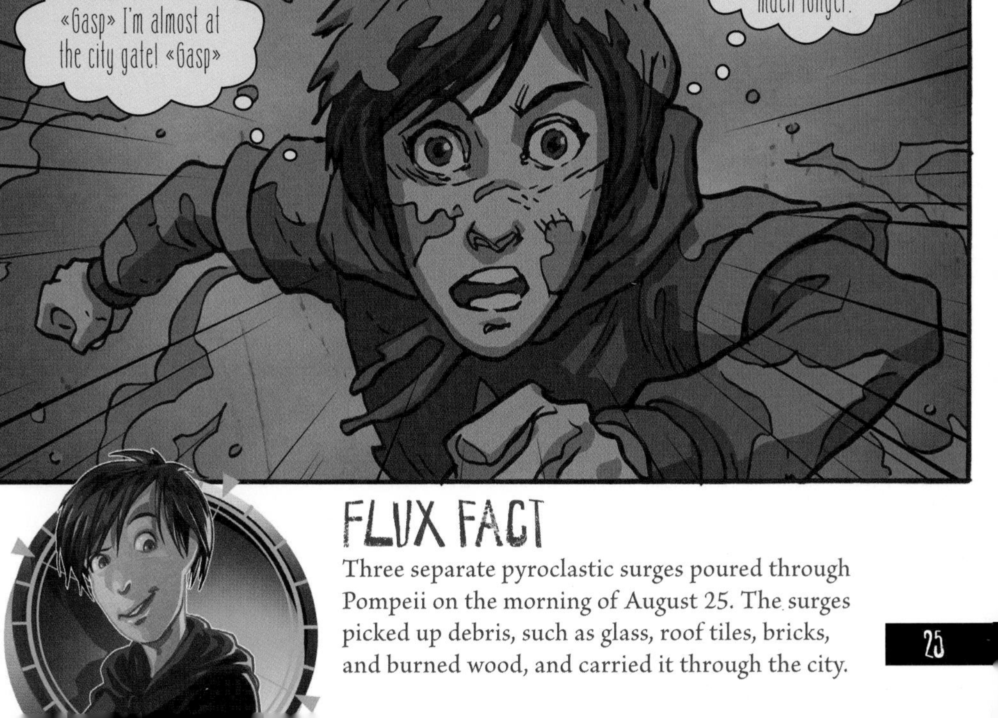

FLUX FACT

Three separate pyroclastic surges poured through Pompeii on the morning of August 25. The surges picked up debris, such as glass, roof tiles, bricks, and burned wood, and carried it through the city.

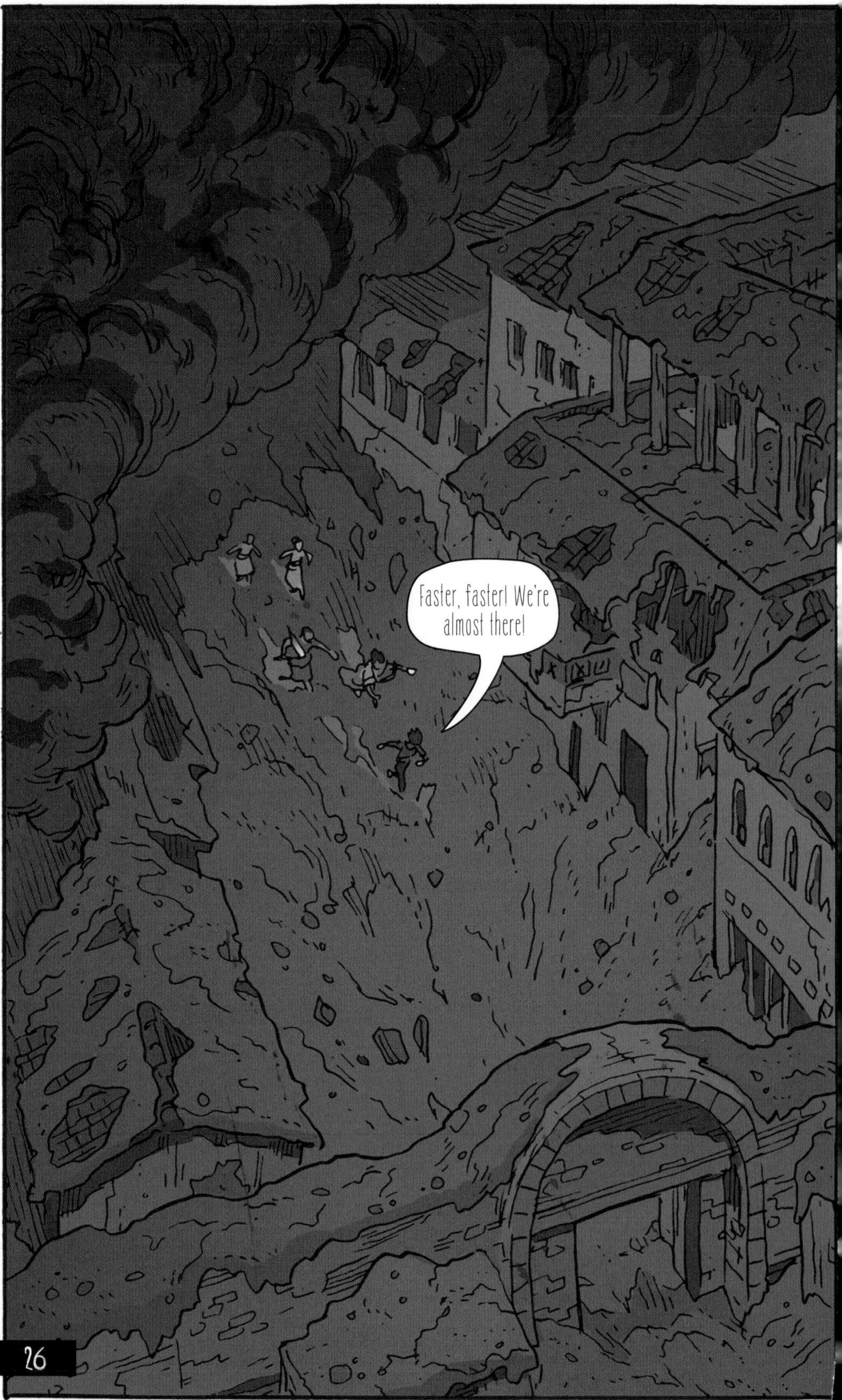
Faster, faster! We're almost there!

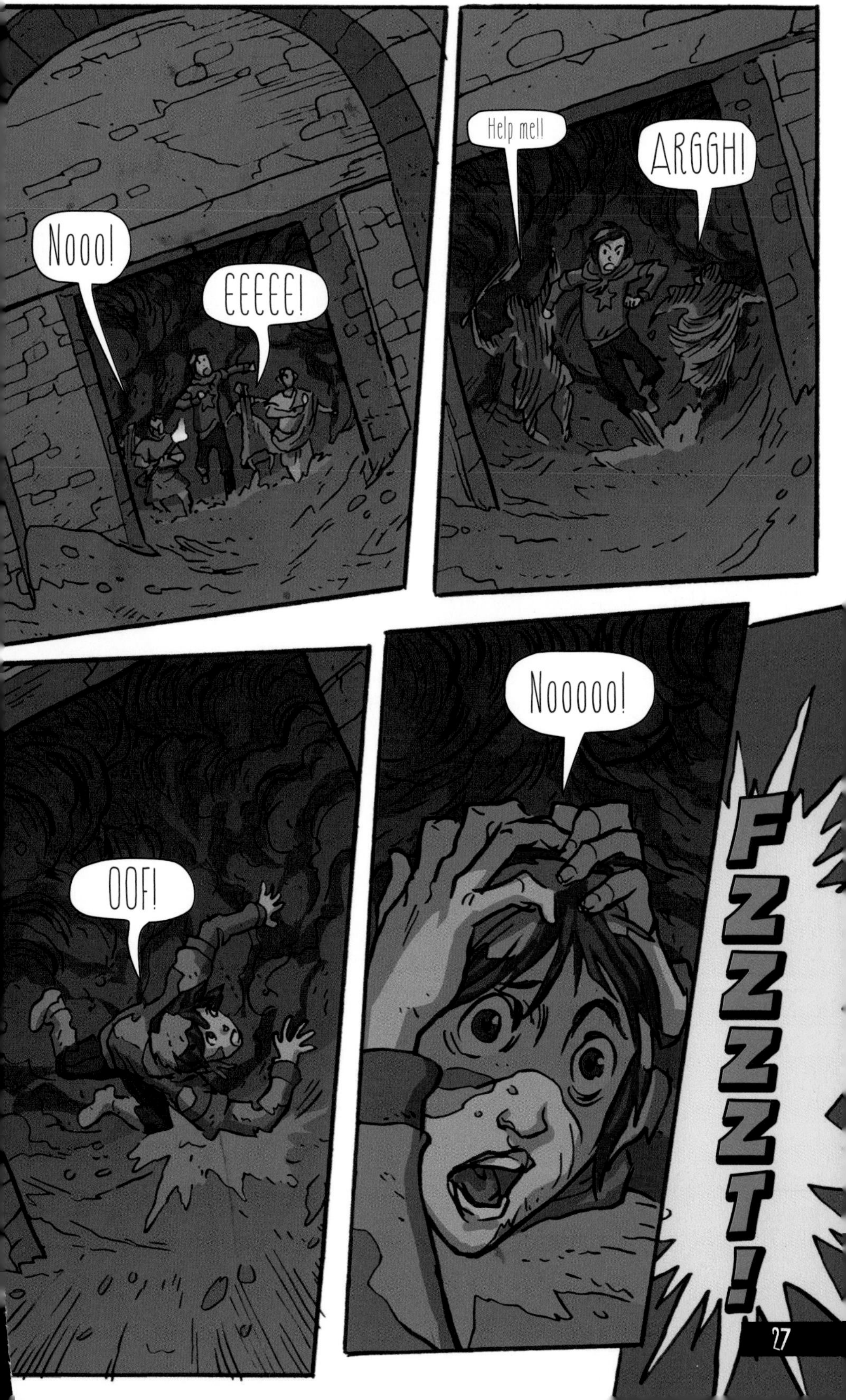

Nooo!
EEEEE!
Help me!!
ARGGH!
OOF!
Nooooo!
FZZZZZT!

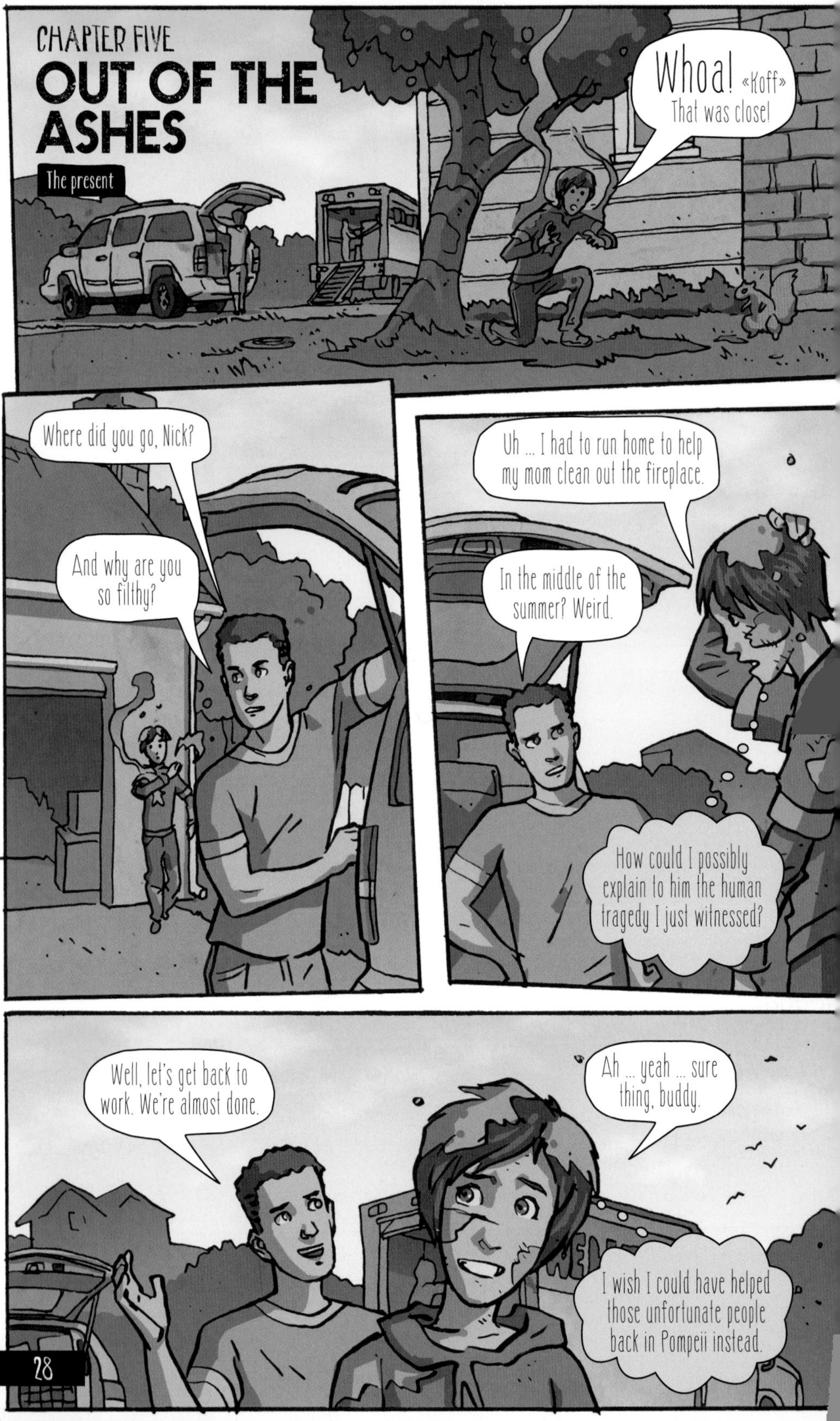
CHAPTER FIVE
OUT OF THE ASHES
The present
Whoa! «Koff» That was close!
Where did you go, Nick?
And why are you so filthy?
Uh ... I had to run home to help my mom clean out the fireplace.
In the middle of the summer? Weird.
How could I possibly explain to him the human tragedy I just witnessed?
Well, let's get back to work. We're almost done.
Ah ... yeah ... sure thing, buddy.
I wish I could have helped those unfortunate people back in Pompeii instead.

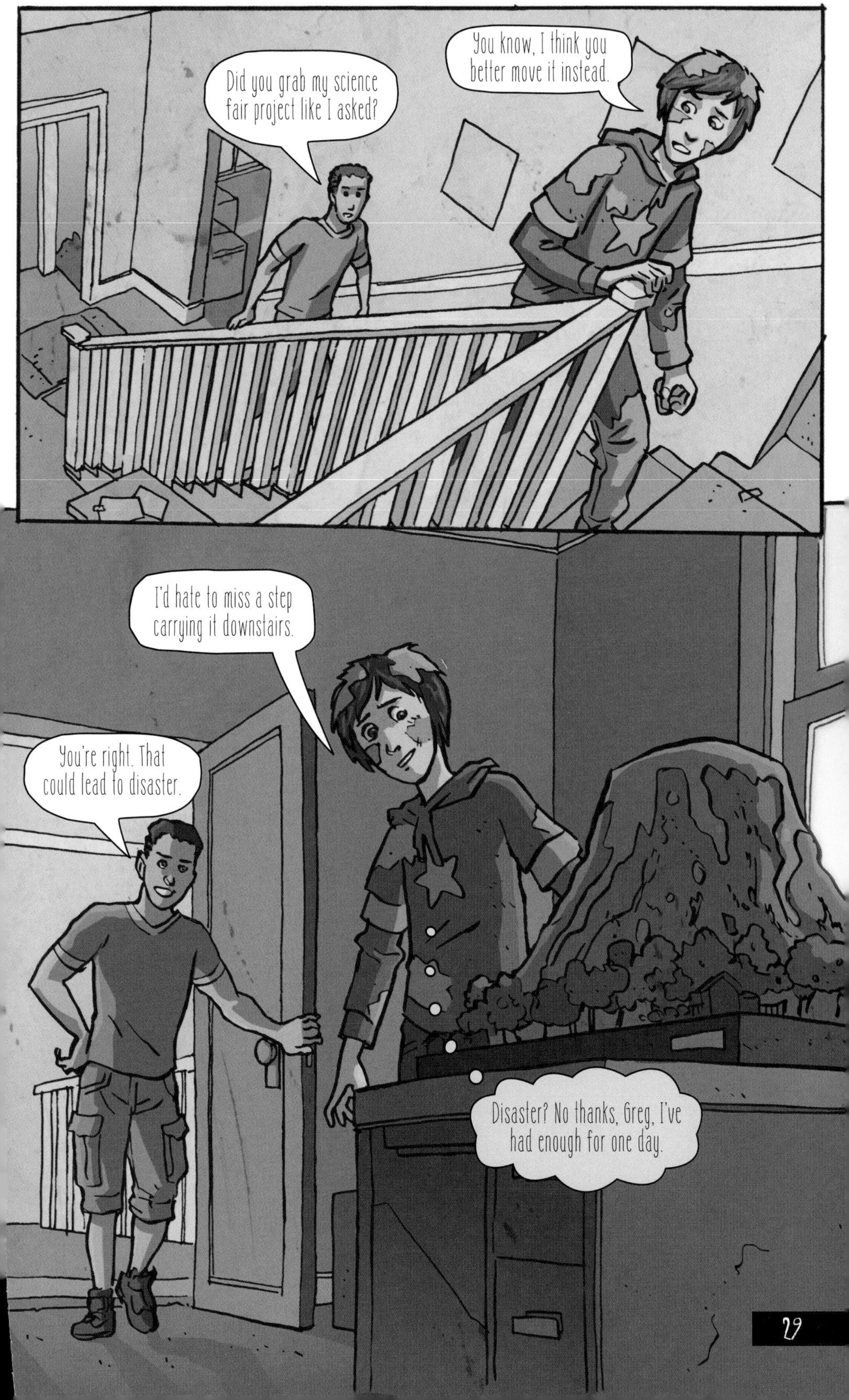
Did you grab my science fair project like I asked?
You know, I think you better move it instead.
I'd hate to miss a step carrying it downstairs.
You're right. That could lead to disaster.
Disaster? No thanks, Greg, I've had enough for one day.

FLUX FILES

PLINY THE YOUNGER

Many details about the eruption of Vesuvius come from a firsthand account by a teenager named Pliny the Younger. Pliny watched Vesuvius erupt from 12 miles (19 km) away in a town called Misenum. His uncle, Pliny the Elder, was a famous navy commander. Elder sailed across the Bay of Naples from Misenum to Pompeii to rescue people. The sea, however, became filled with pumice and ash. He was forced to land in the town of Stabiae, south of Pompeii. There, Elder died from breathing the gases from the eruption.

PLINIAN ERUPTIONS

The eruption of Mount Vesuvius is called a Plinian eruption. This extremely powerful type of volcanic eruption is named for Pliny the Younger. In a Plinian eruption, large columns of gas and volcanic ash shoot high into the sky. Huge amounts of pumice and powerful, constant gas eruptions also occur. The most deadly features of a Plinian eruption are the pyroclastic surges it produces.

HERCULANEUM

The city of Herculaneum was located about 4 miles (6 km) west of Vesuvius when it erupted. The city was destroyed by six pyroclastic surges. They killed every living being that hadn't escaped the city ahead of time.

REDISCOVERING POMPEII

Covered completely in ash, Pompeii was abandoned and forgotten. It was rediscovered in 1599 during digging of an underground water channel. Workers found wall paintings and writings on walls, but the city was not further investigated. The first discovery of a human body was in April 1748. In the following years, more bodies, coins, gems, gold jewelry, and silver plates were uncovered.

VICTIMS OF POMPEII

Scientists and archaeologists have discovered about 1,150 bodies in Pompeii. About 500 more could still be buried in parts of the town that have not been unearthed. Not a single person who stayed in Pompeii during the eruption is known to have survived.

PLASTER CASTS

Archaeologists can study the final moments of people trapped in Pompeii during the eruption. The ash that covered their bodies hardened into rock. Inside the rock, the remains decomposed. Perfect molds formed in the shapes of their bodies. Scientists have injected plaster into these molds to create casts of the victims. Many of the casts are on display in museums and at the ruins of Pompeii.

GLOSSARY

ARCHAEOLOGIST (ar-kee-OL-uh-jist)—a person who learns about the past by digging up old buildings or objects and studying them

COMMERCIAL (kuh-MUHR-shuhl)—to do with buying and selling things

DECOMPOSE (dee-kuhm-POHZ)—to rot or decay

EARTHQUAKE (UHRTH-kwayk)—a sudden, violent shaking of the ground; earthquakes are caused by shifting of Earth's crust

ERUPT (i-RUHPT)—to suddenly burst; a volcano shoots steam, lava, and ash into the air when it erupts

PUMICE (PUHM-iss)—a light, grayish volcanic rock

PYROCLASTIC SURGE (peye-roh-KLAS-tik SURJ)—a fast-moving mixture of hot gases, ash, and rock from a volcano

VOLCANO (vol-KAY-noh)—a mountain with vents through which molten lava, ash, and gas may erupt

READ MORE

JOHNSON, ROBIN. *Pompeii.* Crabtree Chrome. St. Catherines, Ont.: Crabtree Publishing Company, 2013.

SAMUEL, CHARLIE. *Solving the Mysteries of Pompeii.* Digging into History. New York: Marshall Cavendish Benchmark, 2009.

OXLADE, CHRIS. *100 Things You Should Know About Volcanoes.* 100 Things You Should Know About. Broomall, Penn.: Mason Crest Publishers, 2011.

ROYSTON, ANGELA. *The Science of Volcanoes.* Nature's Wrath, The Science Behind Natural Disasters. New York: Gareth Stevens Publishing, 2013.

WAGNER, HEATHER LEHR. *Pompeii.* Lost Worlds and Mysterious Civilizations. New York: Chelsea House, 2011.

INTERNET SITES

FactHound offers a safe, fun way to find Internet sites related to this book. All sites on FactHound have been researched by our staff.

Here's all you do:

Visit *www.facthound.com*

Type in this code: 9781491402511

Super-cool stuff!

Check out projects, games and lots more at
www.capstonekids.com

ABOUT THE AUTHOR

Nel Yomtov is a writer of children's nonfiction books and graphic novels. He specializes in writing about history, country studies, science, and biography. Nel has written frequently for Capstone, including other Nickolas Flux adventures such as *Defend Until Death!: Nickolas Flux and the Battle of the Alamo*; *Night of Rebellion!: Nickolas Flux and the Boston Tea Party*; and *Tracking an Assassin!: Nickolas Flux and the Assassination of Abraham Lincoln*. His graphic novel adaptation, *Jason and the Golden Fleece*, published by Stone Arch Books, was a winner of the 2009 Moonbeam Children's Book Award and the 2011 Lighthouse Literature Award. Nel lives in the New York City area.

ALL THE NICKOLAS FLUX ADVENTURES

ARRESTED FOR WITCHCRAFT!
NICKOLAS FLUX
AND THE SALEM WITCH TRIALS

DEFEND UNTIL DEATH!
NICKOLAS FLUX
AND THE BATTLE OF THE ALAMO

Flight to FREEDOM!
NICKOLAS FLUX
AND THE UNDERGROUND RAILROAD

Night of Rebellion!
NICKOLAS FLUX
AND THE BOSTON TEA PARTY

PERIL IN POMPEII!
NICKOLAS FLUX
AND THE ERUPTION OF MOUNT VESUVIUS

STAKE A CLAIM!
NICKOLAS FLUX
AND THE CALIFORNIA GOLD RUSH

READ THEM ALL!

SURPRISE ATTACK!
NICKOLAS FLUX
AND THE ATTACK ON PEARL HARBOR

TRACKING AN ASSASSIN!
NICKOLAS FLUX
AND THE ASSASSINATION OF ABRAHAM LINCOLN

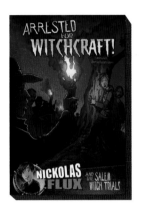

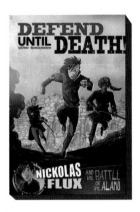

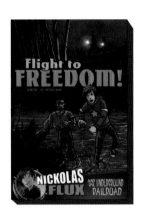

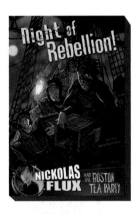

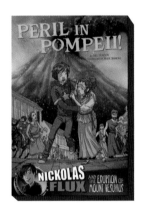

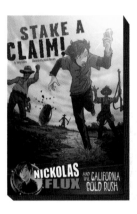

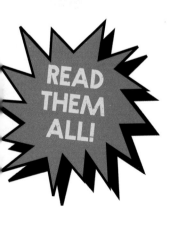

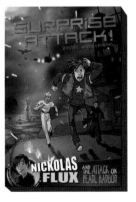

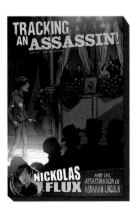